The Blessed Hope

THE BLESSED HOPE

GEORGE ELDON LADD

Professor of New Testament History
and Biblical Theology
Fuller Theological Seminary

WM. B. EERDMANS PUBLISHING COMPANY
Grand Rapids, Michigan

First printing, May 1956
Seventh printing, July 1973

ISBN 0-8028-1111-6

PHOTOLITHOPRINTED BY GRAND RAPIDS BOOK MANUFACTURERS, INC.
GRAND RAPIDS, MICHIGAN

INTRODUCTION

At the heart of Biblical redemptive truth is the Blessed Hope of the personal, glorious second advent of Jesus Christ. Salvation has to do both with the redemption of men as individuals and as a society. Salvation of individual believers includes the "redemption of the body" (Rom. 8:23). We must not only be saved from the guilt of sin, and delivered from the power of sin. Redemption is not completed until we are delivered from the very effects of sin in our mortal bodies. The Biblical doctrine of the resurrection is a redemptive truth: it means the salvation of the body. This salvation will be realized only by the personal second coming of Christ.

Redemption also includes society. God's redemptive purpose involves not only the salvation of individuals; God has a purpose and a goal for mankind as a society inhabiting the earth. The Bible teaches that throughout the entire course of this age, the power and reign of Satan manifests itself not only in the sinfulness and the physical sufferings and mortality of individuals, but also in the evils of corporate historical experience. Satan offered to our Lord authority over the nations, "for it hath been delivered unto me; and to whomsoever I will I give it" (Luke 4:6). While God is sovereign and Satan can do nothing apart from the will of God, there is truth in this declaration of the Evil One. God has permitted Satan to exercise his power in human history. Our generation has witnessed diabolical evils which the preceding generation would have said were impossible for enlightened, civilized men. The demonic element in history is increasingly manifesting itself.

God will not permit Satan to exercise his power in human history forever. Man will not destroy himself from the face of the earth, nor will this planet become a cold, lifeless star. The day is surely coming when the knowledge of God shall cover the earth as the waters cover the sea, when peace and righteousness shall prevail instead of war and evil. The day is surely coming when God will take the reins of government into His hands and the kingdom of God will come on earth and His will be done even as it is in heaven. This glorious destiny for man will be achieved only by the personal, visible, glorious return of Christ. He is destined to be Lord of lords and King of kings. The second coming of Jesus Christ is an absolutely indispensable doctrine in the Biblical teaching of redemption. Apart from His glorious return, God's work will forever be incomplete. At the center of redemption past is Christ on the cross; at the center of redemption future is Christ returning in glory.

There have been eras in the history of the Church when this precious truth has been lost sight of. In the middle ages, the reign of the Catholic Church was thought to be identical with the reign of Christ. At other times, earnest Christians have taught that the true Church through the preaching of the Gospel was to win the entire earth and thus inaugurate the kingdom of God without the personal return of Christ.

In our day among evangelical churches, the doctrine of the second coming of Christ generally receives a wholesome and Biblical emphasis. The interpretation of the book of Revelation which scholars call "futurism" is widely held, and the author is convinced that this is the correct view. The main features of this system of prophetic truth are as follows. The manifestations of evil which have marked human history will at the end of the age be concentrated in one final incarnation of evil, a "super-man," the Antichrist, who will exercise a world-wide rule, deify the state and achieve a union of church and state so that men will be forced to worship him or suffer economic sanctions and death. Antichrist, energized by satanic powers, will especially direct his hostility against God and the people of

God. During his ascendency, there will befall God's people the most fearful persecution history has witnessed. This time of suffering is called the "Great Tribulation," and will be of three and a half years duration. However, God will not be inactive, and during the final period of the Tribulation, God will manifest impending judgment by the outpouring of divine wrath upon the Antichrist and those who worship him.

Another important element in these end times is God's treatment of the Jewish people. They are destined to be restored; the veil will be taken from their minds and they will turn at last as a people in faith to Jesus as their Messiah. Refusing to worship Antichrist, they will become the object of his anger and will suffer fearful martyrdom.

While Antichrist will prevail temporarily, his reign will be short. Christ will return personally and visibly in power and glory to inflict punishment upon Antichrist along with those who have worshipped him, to deliver His people from the midst of tribulation, and to establish His millennial kingdom upon the earth.

In this outline of prophetic teaching, the kingdom of God in its outward manifestation will not come until the Lord Jesus returns in glory. The present mission of the Church is not to save the world and thus establish the kingdom of God but to evangelize the world by the proclamation of the Gospel. The second coming of Christ is thus both the Blessed Hope of the Church and the hope of human history. His coming will mean both salvation and judgment. To this glorious truth the author steadfastly holds; it may be designated by the term *premillennialism*. That this Biblical pattern of prophetic truth has become so widely accepted among our evangelical churches is due in good part to the fact that during the last decades of the nineteenth century, God raised up a group of devout students of the Word to place a new emphasis upon the Blessed Hope. These men have exercised a profound influence for the study of the Word of God and a love for prophetic truth. This has meant essentially a return to the interpretation which prevailed throughout the first centuries of the history of the Christian Church.

However, the program of prophetic events which they taught included important elements which are not found in the early church. Among these were the teachings of the Rapture of the Church at the beginning of the Tribulation and the expectation of an any-moment secret coming of Christ for the purpose of rapturing the Church. Since the coming of Christ would precede the appearance of Antichrist and the Tribulation, it would be unheralded by any preceding signs and could therefore occur at any moment after His ascension to heaven. The coming of Christ is "imminent"; i.e., it can take place at any moment. "Imminence" means that no prophesied event must take place before Christ's return to rapture the Church.

We may designate this teaching by the word *pretribulationism*, because it teaches a pretribulation rapture of the Church so that it escapes the Tribulation. Premillennialism and pretribulationism hold much in common. Both look for a personal Antichrist. Both expect a short period of fearful tribulation at the end of the age. Both are looking for the glorious coming of Christ to establish His millennial kingdom. Pretribulationism adds several other features which are not essential to the main outlines of premillennial truth. Thus premillennialism and pretribulationism are not synonymous. All pretribulationists will be premillennialists, but not all premillennialists will be pretribulationists. Many premillennialists believe that the Scriptures do not teach that Christ will return secretly to rapture the Church before the Tribulation. However, this teaching has been spread widely throughout American Fundamentalism through the godly influence of such men as James M. Gray, A. C. Gaebelein, R. A. Torrey, W. B. Riley, I. M. Haldeman, H. A. Ironside, L. S. Chafer, and many others.

No instrument has been more influential than the Scofield Reference Bible in implanting this view in the thinking of millions of Christians. Most of the Bible schools which have trained a host of young people in the Word of God have been devoted to this pattern of prophetic teaching, and the prophetic conference movement along with many summer Bible conferences has propagated this view. So deeply intrenched has it become that many pastors and Christian leaders have been led to assume that this teaching has been an essential doctrine in the history of the Church extending back to apostolic times and has prevailed widely in all ages among believers who have had a sincere love for the Word of God and who have cherished the Blessed Hope of Christ's return.

During the first half of the present century, occasional voices were raised within the circle of premillennial interpretation in defense of a modification of some of the details of this prophetic program. Honored leaders such as Robert Cameron, W. J. Erdman, Rowland Bingham and Henry Frost were compelled from their further study of the Word to dissent from pretribulationism. Holding steadfastly to the premillennial coming of Christ to establish His kingdom, they felt they could no longer accept the teaching of a secret return of Christ to rapture the Church before the Tribulation. If the Tribulation were to precede Christ's return, it was obvious that the doctrine of an any-moment coming was impossible. Some of these men were sharply criticized for their deviation from the teaching of an any-moment coming of Christ to remove the Church from the world before the Tribulation begins. They were nevertheless recognized to be men of God who were true to the Gospel and unswerving in their defense of the faith once delivered to the saints, and men who loved His appearing. Although they were thought to be in error in their teaching about the Rapture and the Tribulation, this deviation was not considered to be ground for attacking their essential soundness, orthodoxy, and loyalty to the Word of God.

Recently the question has assumed a somewhat different complexion. Within premillennial circles there have been few voices raised on behalf of any view except that of a pretribulation eschatology. The great majority of premillennialists have been also pretribulationists. However, the author is personally acquainted with a good number of Christian leaders who are posttribulationists, but they have not been led to speak or to write in defense of their understanding of the Word. At the same time, there has grown up a large literature both in books and religious magazines devoted to pretribulationism. The modern prophetic conference movement has selected its speakers from the circle of pretribulationists, and any deviating point of view is seldom heard.

As a result there has been a growing tendency among premillennialists to feel that this teaching is identical with pretribulationism and that a theology to be conservative must include the teaching of the Rapture of the Church before the Tribulation. Some Christian institutions and leaders appear to be genuinely fearful that any deviation from a pretribulation eschatology is a step toward liberalism. Schools or Bible teachers which are not pretribulationist are accused of departing from a Biblical faith. We have come even to the point where serious evangelical scholars in their published writings defend a pretribulation eschatology by the accusation that anything less smacks of liberalism.

These are serious matters. If indeed the Word of God clearly and unambiguously teaches the Rapture of the Church before the Tribulation in as distinct terms as it teaches the bodily, visible, glorious second coming of Christ, then such a doctrine must of course be considered as an essential element in conservative theology. If, however, the teaching of a pretribulation rapture is an unnecessary inference and not a clear affirmation of the Word of God, then men may be free to accept or reject it, depending upon the apparent validity of the inference and the degree to which it has the support of Scripture. To make such an inference an essential element of doctrine would only split churches, schools, and Christian institutions and would label a great host of men who are utterly unswerving in their defense of the Word of God and who love and teach the truth of the Lord's coming as men who are tainted with unbelief.

The present book has been written because a number of Christian leaders have expressed the need for a fresh statement on this subject which would consider both points of view. There are many Christians, both laymen and pastors, who are earnestly seeking light. They wish to hear what can be said on the other side for they are not satisfied with the usual pretribulationism.

The central thesis of this book is that *the Blessed Hope is the second coming of Jesus Christ and not a pretribulation rapture.* The Blessed Hope is not synonymous with pretribulationism. Many who hold a pretribulation rapture feel that the coming of Christ cannot be a Blessed Hope if the Church must go through the Great Tribulation. Is not the Blessed Hope the hope of deliverance from tribulation? Who wants to suffer the terrible experiences of those awful days? The question is not, what do we want, but, what does the Word of God teach? No one *wants* to take the Church through the Tribulation. No one is looking and praying for tribulation. How then can one look for the coming of Christ, how can it be a Blessed Hope if it is to be preceded by tribulation? Pretribulationists insist that those who expect the coming of the Lord to rapture the Church only at the end of the Tribulation really cannot have a Blessed Hope.

Such a line of reasoning is persuasive; but if it happens not to agree with the teachings of Scripture, it is dangerous for that very reason. Persuasiveness is no authority; the one question must be, what does the Word of God teach?

This book is written to study that question and to point out that the Word of God does not make the Blessed Hope synonymous with a pretribulation rapture. The Blessed Hope is the coming of the Lord, whether that glorious event occurs before or after the Tribulation.

The Blessed Hope is not deliverance from the Tribulation; it is union with the Lord at His coming.

In carrying out our purpose, it will be necessary to devote much of our discussion to a careful examination of the teaching of pretribulationism. Does the Word of God actually teach that the Church will be raptured before the Tribulation? To answer this question, we must look at the reasons usually given to support pretribulationism. It will perhaps appear to some of our readers that the approach is negative. But this is necessary in the nature of the case. If the Scriptures teach pretribulationism, posttribulationism is impossible. But if the Scriptures do not really teach pretribulationism, then the natural result is a posttribulation position. (We may be permitted to assume that so-called "midtribulationism" is a variant of pretribulationism). The author trusts that this study will not be interpreted primarily as an attack on pretribulationists or pretribulationism. It is not his desire to attack anyone, but to encourage devout study of the Word of God. Several of the author's colleagues at The Fuller Theological Seminary devoutly hold a pretribulation position, and two of them have contributed helpful criticisms and valuable suggestions to this study. The author certainly is not attacking them, nor any others who hold the same position.

Because of this irenic purpose, the names of authors and the sources of quotations of those who hold a different position have usually been omitted. Since the book is designed to help laymen as well as pastors in their study of the Scripture, the paraphernalia and jargon of scholarship have been laid aside and technical questions have been avoided as far as possible.

We have frequently quoted from pretribulation writers, but we trust always in a kindly and generous spirit. In fact, one of the main objectives of the book is to promote courteous discussion of the problem. We would set forth the claim that those who hold that the Scripture teaches that the Church will be raptured only at the end of the Tribulation should have full liberty to hold that position, even as we would allow others the right to hold a pretribulation rapture. For the most part, the Word of God is not explicit about the order of events. Matthew 24 says nothing about the resurrection; the book of Revelation says nothing about the Rapture of the Church; Paul's epistles say nothing about the resurrection of the unrighteous. Our problems arise when we begin to ask questions which were not in the minds of the authors.

We hold that pretribulationism is an inference and not the explicit teaching of the Word of God. Therefore, it is not to be identified with the Blessed Hope. Furthermore, we feel it is not a necessary inference, but is a view which has arisen in comparatively modern times in light of which Scripture has been interpreted. We do not expect pretribulationists to agree with the interpretation of Scripture here set forth, but we do trust them to permit us the right to differ "in the Lord."

One thing should be emphasized: the author would affirm his belief in the personal, premillennial second advent of Jesus Christ. He is looking for His coming; it is his Blessed Hope. His pulpit ministry has continually sounded the expectation and the necessity of the Lord's glorious return. His teaching ministry has placed great emphasis upon the fact that theology is incomplete without the personal coming of Christ to complete the work of redemption. One of the main objectives of an earlier book was to defend premillennialism. However, pretribulationism is not identical with premillennialism; and this book is sent forth with the earnest prayer that it may be used by the Holy Spirit to bring a better understanding to a difficult subject and to promote Christian liberty in the interpretation of prophetic truth. Until "we all attain unto the unity of the faith," until we see "face to face" when we "shall know fully even as [we are] fully known," we must ever hold the truth in love, "giving diligence to keep the unity of the Spirit in the bond of peace."

CONTENTS

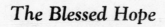

The Blessed Hope

1

THE HISTORIC HOPE OF THE CHURCH

THE QUESTION of the relationship of the Rapture to that of the Tribulation may be set in proper perspective if we first survey the history of prophetic interpretation. The hope of the Church throughout the early centuries was the second coming of Christ, not a pretribulation rapture. If the Blessed Hope is in fact a pretribulation rapture, then the Church has never known that hope through most of its history, for the idea of a pretribulation rapture did not appear in prophetic interpretation until the nineteenth century.

Pretribulationists are reluctant to admit this. Books which defend this pattern of prophetic teaching frequently try to show that it is an ancient teaching extending all the way back to apostolic times. They usually seek proof in the assertion that the early fathers believed in the imminence of Christ's return. If the return of Christ was an event for which men were looking — so the argument runs — then the coming of Christ was expected to occur at any moment, i.e., before the Tribulation and before Antichrist appeared. In this chapter, we shall trace the broad outlines of the history of prophetic interpretation with reference to the Church and the Tribulation to discover whether a pretribulation rapture was an element in the hope of the Church.

Let it be at once emphasized that we are not turning to the church fathers to find authority for either pre- or posttribulationism. The one authority is the Word of God, and we are not confined in the strait-jacket of tradition. Our purpose is to place this question in a proper historical

19

perspective, inasmuch as some teachers claim that pre-tribulationism is an ancient and honorable doctrine and one which is necessary for Christian faith. While tradition does not provide authority, it would nevertheless be difficult to suppose that God had left His people in ignorance of an essential truth for nineteen centuries.

The early church lived in expectation of Christ's return. "Ye perceive how in a little time the fruit of a tree comes to maturity. Of a truth, soon and suddenly shall His will be accomplished, as the Scripture also bears witness, saying, 'Speedily will He come and will not tarry,' and 'The Lord shall suddenly come to His temple, even the Holy One, for whom ye look' " (I Clement 23). To deduce from this attitude of expectancy a belief in a pretribulation rapture and an any-moment coming of Christ, as has often been done, is not sound. The expectation of the coming of Christ *included the events which would attend and precede His coming.* The early fathers who emphasized an attitude of expectancy believed that this entire complex of events — Antichrist, tribulation, return of Christ — would soon occur. This is not the same as an any-moment coming of Christ.

The Didache

This is proven by the teaching of one of the earliest pieces of Christian literature after the New Testament, the so-called Didache, a piece of Christian instruction dating from the first quarter of the second century. The last chapter is devoted to exhortations in view of the woes expected at the end of the world. The author urges an attitude of watching in view of the uncertainty of the time of the end. "Watch over your life; let your lamps be not quenched and your loins be not ungirded, but be ready, for you know not the hour in which your Lord cometh" (16.1). This language, however, cannot be taken to mean an "any-moment rapture," for the author proceeds to sketch the consummation of the age in which he warns the Church against the peril of falling away from the faith when Antichrist appears. There "shall appear the deceiver of the world as a Son of God, and shall do signs and wonders and the earth shall be given over into his hands and he shall commit iniquities which have never been since the world began. Then shall the creation of mankind come to the fiery trial and many shall be offended and be lost, but they who endure in their faith shall be saved by the curse itself. And then shall appear the signs of the truth. First the sign spread out in Heaven, then the sign of the trumpet, and thirdly the resurrection of the dead: but not of all the dead, but as it was said, The Lord shall come and all his saints with him. Then shall the world see the Lord coming on the clouds of Heaven."

The Didachist looks forward to the appearance of Antichrist who will rule the world and inflict men with severe persecution. The many who are to be offended and be lost are professing Christians who do not stand true; for only those who endure in their faith shall be saved. (The meaning of the phrase "by the curse itself" is unknown.) After the Tribulation will appear signs of the end, the final sign being the resurrection of the righteous. Then at last the Lord will come, bringing with Him the saints who have died. The purpose of the Didachist in writing this exhortation was to prepare the Church for the Great Tribulation and the sufferings to be inflicted by the Antichrist, and to urge steadfastness; "for the whole time of your faith shall not profit you except ye be found perfect at the last time."

While the author of the Didache emphasized the spirit of expectancy and watchfulness in view of the uncertainty of the time of the coming of Christ, he expects the Church to suffer at the hands of Antichrist during the Great Tribulation, and he expects the coming of Christ to occur only at the end of this time of woe.

Barnabas

A second piece of Christian literature which is really anonymous bears the title "The Epistle of Barnabas." It stems from about the same period as the Didache. The author of this little tract is looking not only for the second coming of Christ but also for the last time of trouble. He warns believers to seek out earnestly those things which are able to save them, and to flee from all the works of lawlessness and to hate the era of this present time that they might be loved in that which is to come. They are to shun fellowship with sinners and wicked men, for "the final stumblingblock is at hand of which it was written, as Enoch says, 'For to this end the Lord has cut short the times and the days, that his beloved should make haste and come to his inheritance' " (4.3). This means that the Antichrist is at hand, but the Lord will cut short the time of the Tribulation that His Beloved — the Lord Jesus — might make haste and return to His people. According to this, Barnabas expected the Church to go through the Tribulation and Christ to return only at its termination. This is again asserted in 15.5: "When his Son comes, he will destroy the time of the wicked one and will judge the godless, and will change the sun and moon and the stars, and then he will truly rest on the seventh day." The second coming of Christ will destroy the wicked one, the Antichrist; and if so, the appearance of Antichrist is expected to precede the Lord's return.

That Barnabas could not have looked for an any-moment return of Christ is proven by his expectation that the end would not come until the Roman empire should fall. "Ten kingdoms shall reign upon the earth and there shall rise up after them a little king, who shall subdue three of the kings under one" (4.4). Antichrist would arise after the Roman empire had broken down into ten kingdoms. This obviously could not occur at once, for in the first century Rome's might and stability was at its apex.

The Shepherd of Hermas

An expression appears in the Shepherd of Hermas (cir. 150 A. D.) which has been claimed by pretribulationists to teach a pretribulation rapture. The words are, "If then you are prepared beforehand, and repent with all your hearts toward the Lord, you will be able to escape it, if your heart be made pure and blameless, and you serve the Lord blamelessly for the rest of the days of your life. Go then and tell the Lord's elect ones of His great deeds, and tell them that this beast is the type of the great persecution which is to come" (Vision 4,2,5). When this phrase is lifted out of its context, it might be understood to teach some such idea as that of a rapture from tribulation. However, when one reads the entire passage, he finds that the exact opposite is taught, for the author is referring to preservation in and through tribulation.

Hermas was walking down the road and met a fearful monster like a leviathan with fiery locusts going out of its mouth, about a hundred feet in size, with four colors on its head: black, blood red, gold, and white. Hermas began to pray to the Lord to rescue him from the beast, but instead he was reminded of his faith in the Lord and the great things he had been taught. Then boldly he faced the beast head-on, and after the beast rushed at him as though it would destroy a city, it came near and stretched itself out on the ground and put forth nothing except its tongue, and did not move at all until Hermas passed it by.

The beast was a symbol of the Great Tribulation to come. The escape promised was not deliverance from the presence of tribulation, but preservation in the presence of tribulation. This is proven by the interpretation of the four colors. Black means the world, fiery red means the destruction of the world, gold represents the Church purified by fire, and white means the world to come. Here we have a teaching common in the early church that tribulation effects purity. "The golden part is you, who have fled from this world, for even as gold is 'tried in the fire' and becomes valuable, so also you who live among them [that is, the fire and blood of tribulation] are being tried. Those then who remain and pass through the flames shall be purified by them." "Therefore do not cease to speak to the ears of the saints. You have also the type of the great persecution to come, but if you will [warn them] it shall be nothing." Hermas is admonished to prepare the Church for the Tribulation, to warn that it is God's purpose to purify the Church by the fiery trial of persecution. If the Church is prepared, it need not fear the sufferings to come; they will be as nothing to those whose faith is fixed in the Lord.

Justin Martyr

One of the earliest fathers (cir. 150) who was an avowed premillennialist was Justin Martyr. He makes only passing reference to Antichrist, but this reference proves that Justin expected the Church to go through the Tribulation and to be persecuted by Antichrist. Speaking of Christ's second advent, he says: "He shall come from heaven with glory, when the man of apostasy, who speaks strange things against the Most High, shall venture to do unlawful deeds on the earth against us Christians, who, having learned the true worship of God from the law, and the word which went forth from Jerusalem by means of the apostles of Jesus, have fled for safety to the God of Jacob and the God of Israel." Justin has no fear of this coming Tribulation, for he says, "Now it is evident that no one can terrify or subdue us who have believed in Jesus over all the world. For it is plain that, though beheaded, and crucified, and thrown to wild beasts, and chains, and fire, and all other kinds of torture, we do not give up our confession; but the more such things happen, the more do others and in larger numbers become faithful, and worshippers of God through the name of Jesus" (Dialogue with Trypho, 110). Justin, who himself became a martyr, feels that the sufferings to be inflicted by the "man of apostasy," the Antichrist, will

be little worse than what Christians were already gladly
and fearlessly suffering for Christ.

Irenaeus

The first of the church fathers who devotes an extensive
discussion to the coming of Antichrist and the Great Tribulation is Irenaeus, Bishop of Lyons in the late second. century A. D. Irenaeus was a thoroughgoing premillenarian,
the first, in fact, to give us a premillennial system of interpretation; but he did not believe in an any-moment coming
of Christ and a rapture of the Church before the Tribulation and coming of Antichrist. On the contrary, he looked
forward to a series of significant historical events within
the Roman empire before Antichrist could arise and Christ
return. "In a still clearer light has John, in the Apocalypse,
indicated to the Lord's disciples what shall happen in the
last times, and concerning the ten kings who shall then
arise, among whom the empire which now rules [the earth]
shall be partitioned. He teaches us what the ten horns shall
be which were seen by Daniel, telling us that thus it had
been said to him [see Rev. 17:12]. It is manifest, therefore, that of these [potentates], he who is to come shall
slay three, and subject the remainder to his power, and
that he shall be himself the eighth among them. And they
shall lay Babylon waste, and burn her with fire, and shall
give their kingdom to the beast, and. put the church to
flight. After that they shall be destroyed by the coming
of our Lord" (Against Heresies, 5,26,1).

Three important points are to be noted in Irenaeus' expectation of the future. First, he does not believe that the
end is immediately at hand. A little further on he warns
the Church against teachers who are propagating false
views about the identity of the Antichrist. Like Barnabas,
he urges them rather to await the division of the kingdom
into ten parts which must occur before Antichrist can
arise. Rather than expecting an immediate end, men are
to await the fulfillment of these prophesies.

Second, Antichrist, when he appears, will put the Church to flight. Speaking of this tribulation which will befall the Church at the hands of Antichrist, Irenaeus says, "And for this cause tribulation is necessary for those who are saved, that having been after a manner broken up, and rendered fine, and sprinkled over by the patience of the Word of God, and set on fire [for purification], they may be fitted for the royal banquet" (27,4). Again, as in Hermas, God is expected to use the Great Tribulation to accomplish the purification of the Church.

Third, the second coming of Christ will take place at the end of the Tribulation to destroy the Antichrist and to deliver His Church. "But when this Antichrist shall have devastated all things in this world, he will reign for three years and six months, and sit in the temple at Jerusalem; and then the Lord will come from heaven in the clouds, in the glory of the Father, sending this man [Antichrist] and those who follow him into the lake of fire; but bringing in for the righteous [the Church] the times of the kingdom" (30,4). At this time the resurrection of the saints and the rapture of the living saints will take place. "For all those, and other words, were unquestionably spoken in reference to the resurrection of the just, which takes place after the coming of the Antichrist, and the destruction of all nations under his rule; in (the times of) which (resurrection) the righteous shall reign on the earth, waxing stronger by the sight of the Lord: and through Him they shall become accustomed to partake in the glory of God the Father, and shall enjoy in the kingdom intercourse and communion with the holy angels, and union with spiritual beings; and (with respect to) those whom the Lord shall find in the flesh, awaiting Him from heaven, and who have suffered tribulation, as well as escaped the hands of the Wicked one" (35,1).

In this first detailed outline of prophetic events after the New Testament, Irenaeus looks for the overthrow of Rome and the division of the Empire among ten kings. Then Antichrist will appear and will kill three of the ten and rule over the other seven. Antichrist will direct his wrath particularly against the Church and put her to flight, but God will use the Tribulation to purify the Church. After three and a half years, Christ will return in glory to punish Antichrist, raise the dead saints, and bring the living saints, both those who have suffered persecution by Antichrist and those who have escaped his anger, into the millennial kingdom.

Tertullian

Along with Justin Martyr and Irenaeus, another avowed premillennialist was Tertullian of North Africa of the late second and third centuries. "But we do confess that a kingdom is promised to us upon the earth, although before heaven, only in another state of existence; inasmuch as it will be after the resurrection for a thousand years in the divinely built city of Jerusalem" (Adv. Marcion 3,25). In one passage, Tertullian writes as though he believed in an any-moment coming of Christ. "But what a spectacle is that fast approaching advent of our Lord, now owned by all, now highly exalted, now a triumphant one!" (The Shows, 30).

However, Tertullian cannot be designated a pretribulation rapturist. He did not look for a restoration of the Jews to their land and a time of tribulation which would primarily concern the restored Israel. "As for the restoration of Judea, however, which even the Jews themselves, induced by the names of the places and countries, hope for just as it is described, it would be tedious to state at length how the figurative interpretation is spiritually applicable to Christ and His church, and to the character and fruits thereof" (Adv. Marcion, 3,25). Furthermore, Tertullian believed that the end could not come at any moment but would be heralded by signs of warning. In his tractate "On the Resurrection of the Flesh" (22), Tertullian speaks of directing his prayers "toward the end of this world, to the

passing away thereof at the great day of the Lord — of
His wrath and vengeance — the last day, which is hidden
(from all), and known to none but the Father, although
announced before hand by signs and wonders, and the dissolution of the elements, and the conflict of nations." After
describing some of the heavenly signs which would an-
nounce the coming of the end, Tertullian quotes the Biblical
exhortation, " 'Watch ye, therefore, and pray always, that
ye may be accounted worthy to escape all those things, and
to stand before the Son of man'; that is, no doubt, at the
resurrection, after all these things have been previously
transacted." The object of Tertullian's hope and prayers is
not a secret any-moment coming of the Lord to rapture the
Church; it is the hope of standing before the Son of man
after a series of cosmic signs have appeared and "all of
these things have taken place." He places this event at the
day of the Lord and the resurrection of the dead at the end
of a series of preceding signs and events.

Lactantius

Lactantius was a Latin father of the late third and early
fourth centuries who devoted considerable attention in his
"Divine Institutes" to the coming of Antichrist and the
consummation of the age. There is one quotation which, if
taken out of context, might suggest the expectation of an
any-moment rapture. "It is permitted us to know respecting the signs, which are spoken by the prophets, for they
foretold signs by which the consummation of the times is
to be expected by us from day to day, and to be feared"
(7,25). However, it is not the coming of Christ which was
daily expected but the appearance of a series of signs which
would precede the end. Lactantius believed that human
history was to run a six thousand year course and to be
followed by a millennium. Of the six thousand years, there
remained in his day some two hundred years before the end
would come (25).

During this period, profound rearrangements of the political situation must take place. The Roman empire must be taken away from the earth and the government returned to Asia, for the East must again bear rule and the West be reduced to servitude (7,15). Rome was doomed to perish and from the ruins would arise ten kings who would divide the world among them. Only then would appear the Antichrist to reign over the whole world.

Before these final events, a severe deterioration must occur in human society, and Lactantius devotes considerable space to the description of these evil times. So terrible will they be that nine-tenths of the human race will be destroyed. The Church, along with the world, is destined to suffer the evils of the end-times. "Of the worshippers of God also, two parts will perish; and the third part, which shall have been proved, will remain" (7,16). Finally, Antichrist will appear and will terribly afflict the righteous and will rule the earth forty-two months. The righteous will flee from the ravages of Antichrist but will be pursued and surrounded. Then they will call upon God and God will hear them and send a Great King to rescue them and to destroy the wicked with the fire and sword (7,17). This coming of Christ will be preceded by a special sign: "There shall suddenly fall from heaven a sword, that the righteous may know that the leader of the sacred warfare is about to descend" (19). After this, the dead will rise and the world be renewed for the millennial kingdom.

Such an expectation is far removed from that of an any-moment coming of Christ and a deliverance of the Church from the tribulations of the end-times.

Hippolytus

One of the first Christians to give us a treatise on the Antichrist is Hippolytus, a Bishop of Rome during the first decades of the third century A. D. Hippolytus applies the fourth beast of Daniel to the Roman empire then ruling the world, and interprets the ten toes of the image in Daniel 2 of ten kings who would arise out of the Roman empire. This is also symbolized by the ten horns of the fourth beast. The horn which will root up three horns is Antichrist. He is to destroy the kings of Egypt, Libya and Ethiopia, after which he will rule the world and persecute the saints. Hippolytus tentatively suggests that the mark of the Beast, 666, may mean *Latinus,* but he is uncertain. "Wherefore we ought neither to give it out as if this were certainly his name, nor again ignore the fact that he may not be otherwise designated. But having the mystery of God in our heart, we ought in fear to keep faithfully what has been told us by the blessed prophets, in order that when these things come to pass, we may be prepared for them, and not be deceived" (50).

Hippolytus interprets Revelation 12 of "the tribulation of the persecution which is to fall upon the Church from the adversary" (60). There the "saints" are identified as the Christian Church. The time and times and half a time refer "to the one thousand two hundred and three score days (the half of the week) during which the tyrant is to reign and persecute the Church, which flees from city to city, and seeks concealment in the wilderness among the mountains" (61). After the Abomination of Desolation and all of the attendant events, "what remains but the coming of our Lord and Saviour Jesus Christ from heaven, for whom we have looked and hoped? who shall bring the conflagration and just judgment upon all who have refused to believe on Him. For the Lord says, 'And when these things begin to come to pass, then look up, and lift up your heads; for your redemption draweth nigh.' 'And there shall not a hair of your head perish.' 'For as the lightning cometh out of the east, and shineth even unto the west, so shall also the coming of the Son of man be' " (64). After the return of Christ will take place the resurrection and the kingdom of the saints as announced in Revelation 20, and I Thessalonians 4.

In this survey of the early centuries we have found that the Church interpreted the book of Revelation along futurist lines; i.e., they understood the book to predict the eschatological events which would attend the end of the world. The Antichrist was understood to be an evil ruler of the end-times who would persecute the Church, afflicting her with great tribulation. Every church father who deals with the subject expects the Church to suffer at the hands of Antichrist. God would purify the Church through suffering, and Christ would save her by His return at the end of the Tribulation when He would destroy Antichrist, deliver His Church, and bring the world to an end and inaugurate His millennial kingdom. The prevailing view is a posttribulation premillennialism. We can find no trace of pretribulationism in the early church; and no modern pretribulationist has successfully proved that this particular doctrine was held by any of the church fathers or students of the Word before the nineteenth century.

The Middle Ages

After the first centuries, the expectation of an Antichrist as an evil world ruler to appear just before the return of Christ gradually disappeared. Revelation came to be interpreted along spiritual lines, and after the time of Augustine, his "amillennial" view that the thousand years began with Christ's earthly life and would continue to the end of the church age became the predominant interpretation.

During the Middle Ages, the "historical" interpretation of Revelation arose in which the book was thought to give in symbolic form an outline of the history of the Church. Antichrist was frequently interpreted to mean the Saracens, and the false prophet to mean Mohammed. Pope Innocent III made effective use of the Revelation to stir up support for his crusade.

The "Protestant" Interpretation

The Reformers took over this type of historical interpretation of prophetic truth and found in the Antichrist a prophecy of the Papacy. Luther at first felt that Revelation was defective in everything which could be called apostolic or prophetic and was offended by the visions and symbols of the book; but he came to feel that the prophecy was an outline of the whole course of church history and that the Papacy was predicted both in chapters 11 and 12 and in the second beast of chapter 13. The number 666 represented the period of papal domination.

This "historical" type of interpretation with its application of the Antichrist to papal Rome so dominated Protestant study of prophetic truth for three centuries that it has frequently been called "the Protestant" interpretation. Some historical interpreters were premillennialists. They found the history of the Church symbolized in the seals, vials, and trumpets, with the second coming of Christ in chapter 19. After the return of Christ, there would be a millennial reign before the final consummation. We would emphasize that there have been many students of the Word who have been thorough-going premillennialists who shared very little of the outline of prophetic truth which today is called premillenialism. Such were Joseph Mede, Isaac Newton, William Whiston, J. A. Bengel and Henry Alford. These men, and many others, taught the premillennial return of Christ, but they did not believe in a personal Antichrist who would appear at the end of the age to persecute the saints during a three and a half year period of tribulation. Neither did they believe in what we call "the Great Tribulation." They believed that the Tribulation extended throughout the history of the Church, and the three and a half years or twelve hundred and sixty days were frequently interpreted to mean twelve hundred and sixty years of church history before the end times could arrive.

A new and different interpretation was created by Daniel Whitby (1706) who thought that the world was to be completely evangelized and the Church to rule the world. Vitringa (d. 1722) applied this view to the interpretation of the Revelation producing postmillennialism. He followed the historical interpretation for the first nineteen chapters and interpreted the first part of chapter twenty as a future era when the Church would reign over the world after the destruction of anti-Christian Rome. The millennium was thus placed in the future but before the return of Christ; and the meaning of "postmillennialism" is that Christ's return would occur only after the millennial period. One of the most famous exponents of this view was David Brown (1891), one of the co-editors of the widely used Jamieson, Fausset and Brown's *Commentary on the Bible.*

It is obvious that so long as the Roman church and the Papacy were identified with the Antichrist, no idea of a pretribulation rapture could be possible, for in this interpretation the period of tribulation was not 1260 days but 1260 years. Such a view lent itself to date-setting. Whiston predicted that the millennium would begin in 1715. When it failed to occur, he deferred the date to 1734. When he survived both dates, he projected the time to 1766 but did not live to see his prediction fail a third time. Bengel expected the end to come on June 18, 1836.

Many of the great Christians of Reformation and post-Reformation times shared this view of prophetic truth and identified Antichrist with the Roman Papacy. This is a fact which should be well pondered by modern students who insist that a pretribulation eschatology is *essential* to an orthodox theology. Among adherents of this interpretation were the Waldenses, the Hussites, Wyclif, Luther, Calvin, Zwingli, Melanchthon, the Baptist theologian John Gill, the martyrs Cranmer, Tyndale, Latimer and Ridley. John Wesley, following Bengel, thought that the papal Antichrist would be overthrown in 1836 and would be succeeded not only by a millennium but by two millenniums, the first on earth and the second in heaven. Jonathan Ed-

wards held that the fulfillment of the Revelation in the
history of the Church was an unanswerable argument for
the inspiration of the Scriptures. He held that the 1260
years of Revelation began in 606 A. D. and that he was
therefore living in the last days.

Some of these men were premillennialists, but Edwards
adopted the Whitbyan postmillennialism. However, they
all shared the historical view; none of them was a futurist,
looking for a short tribulation with a personal Antichrist
just before the return of Christ. Therefore, the idea of a
pretribulation rapture had no place in their interpretation
of prophecy.

2

THE RISE AND SPREAD OF PRETRIBULATIONISM

IN THE preceding chapter, we traced the broad outlines of the history of prophetic interpretation and found no trace of pretribulationism. The first three centuries were characterized by a futurist, premillennial interpretation but not of the pretribulation type. The Middle Ages forsook this primitive interpretation for either a spiritual interpretation or the historical view. The latter was so widely accepted in the sixteenth, seventeenth and eighteenth centuries that it has been called the "Protestant" view.

The Return to Futurism

With the dawn of the nineteenth century, there occurred a movement which brought about a return to the primitive view and which also gave rise to pretribulationism.

Whitby's new postmillennial view exercised great influence in Europe in the eighteenth century and resulted in a minimizing of the importance of the doctrine of the Lord's return. At the turn of the century, a strong reaction arose which reasserted the importance of the personal coming of Christ and often emphasized the place of the earthly kingdom after the Lord's return. Outstanding among the leaders of this prophetic revival were William Cuninghame, Joshua W. Brooks, Edward Bickersteth, T. R. Birks, and E. B. Elliott — all of whom proclaimed the personal, *premillennial* coming of Christ but continued to follow the historical method of applying the prophecies of Antichrist to the Papacy and interpreting the 1260 days as years.

Many periodicals appeared which were devoted to the exposition of prophecy and to heralding the imminent return of Christ. Most of them experienced only a short life but exercised great influence for a few years. One of these periodicals was *The Investigator* (1831-36), edited by J. W. Brooks, the last volume of which contained a *Dictionary of Writers on the Prophecies* in which Brooks compiled over 2,100 titles of books on prophetic subjects, together with 500 commentaries on books of the Bible. Numerous anonymous tracts appeared bearing such titles as "The End of All Things is at Hand."

Prophetic conferences began to spring up. A wealthy banker, Henry Drummond, sponsored a series of prophetic conferences at his villa at Albury Park from 1826-1830. Drummond's own interpretation was of the historical, premillennial type. To this conference came Edward Irving, an eloquent preacher who expounded prophetic themes to a London congregation of over a thousand drawn from the most brilliant circles of society. Irving later toured Scotland to proclaim the imminence of Christ's coming and there won the Bonar brothers to a millennial view, preaching sometimes to out-door crowds of ten to twelve thousand. It is a tragedy that a young man of such great gifts and promise experienced so sad an end. In 1830, he wrote a tract in which he asserted that Jesus possessed a fallen human nature. Shortly after this, tongues broke out in his congregation. Heresy proceedings were initiated and he was deposed in 1833 and died, broken-hearted, the next year.

Just before Irving attended the Albury meeting, he had come upon a copy of the work on the *Coming of the Messiah* by the Spanish Jesuit, Lacunza (Ben-Ezra). Lacunza had rediscovered the truth of the second advent of Christ to establish His millennial kingdom which had been lost in Catholicism. Even though he was a Catholic, he applied the prophecy of the second beast in Revelation thirteen to a corrupted Roman priesthood. In 1827, this book and the millennial question became the main objects of study at the Albury conference. Lady Powerscourt attended these meetings and became so interested that she established similar meetings at Powerscourt House. It was in these Powerscourt meetings that some of the characteristic doctrines of "Darbyism" can be discovered for the first time.

Out of this revival of interest in prophetic truth came two new interpretations: futurism and "Darbyism."[1] The futuristic interpretation was essentially a return to the method of prophetic truth found in the early fathers, essential to which is the teaching that the Antichrist will be a satanically inspired world-ruler at the end of the age who would inflict severe persecution upon the Church during the Great Tribulation. At the end of the Tribulation, Christ would return to deliver the Church, punish Antichrist, raise the righteous dead, and establish His millennial kingdom. Darbyism modified this outline of truth by teaching a coming of Christ to rapture the Church before the Tribulation and before His coming in glory to establish the millennial kingdom.

The rediscovery of futurism is associated with the names of S. R. Maitland, James Todd, and William Burgh. Before we turn to these men, we should note that a futurist interpretation of prophecy had earlier been recovered within the Roman Catholic Church. It will probably come as a shock to many modern futurists to be told that the first scholar in relatively modern times who returned to the patristic futuristic interpretation was a Spanish Jesuit named Ribera. In 1590, Ribera published a commentary on the Revelation as a counter-interpretation to the prevailing view among Protestants which identified the Papacy with the Antichrist. Ribera applied all of Revelation but the earliest chapters to the end time rather than to the history of the Church. Antichrist would be a single evil person who would be received by the Jews and would

---

1. We do not like the word, but it is useful and not inaccurate because J. N. Darby was associated with the formation of the particular teaching under discussion and became the most influential advocate of these views, especially through his travels and writings. This pattern of prophetic interpretation has now more commonly been designated Dispensationalism, of which pretribulationism is an essential element.

rebuild Jerusalem, abolish Christianity, deny Christ, persecute the Church and rule the world for three and a half years. On one subject, Ribera was not a futurist: he followed the Augustinian interpretation of the millennium in making the entire period between the cross and Antichrist. He differed from Augustine in making the "first resurrection" to refer to the heavenly life of the martyrs when they would reign in heaven with Christ throughout the millennium, i.e., the church age. A number of Catholic scholars espoused this futuristic interpretation of Antichrist, among them Bellarmine, the most notable of the Jesuit controversialists and the greatest adversary of the Protestant churches.

This futurist interpretation with its personal Antichrist and three and a half year period of tribulation did not take root in the Protestant church until the early nineteenth century. The first Protestant to adopt it was S. R. Maitland. He received a legal training but abandoned the profession in 1823 to become a curate. In 1826 he published a pamphlet whose title is self-explanatory: *An Enquiry into the Ground on which the Prophetic Period of Daniel and St. John Has Been Supposed to Consist of 1260 Years.* This small pamphlet was an attack on the year-day theory of the historical interpreters, insisting upon a period of 1260 literal days of tribulation before the return of Christ. The pamphlet resulted in a "paper-war" with the historicists which lasted many years.

James H. Todd, professor of Hebrew at Dublin, met Maitland and became his follower. In 1838 he gave the Donnellan lectures using the subject, *Discourses on the Prophecies Relating to Antichrist in the Writings of Daniel and St. Paul,* dedicating the published lectures to Maitland. This is a detailed study of over five hundred pages on these prophecies. Todd repeatedly refers to Antichrist as "the head and leader of a formidable persecution of the Christian Church," "the great enemy and persecutor of the

Church," and the like. In 1840, he published a second series of studies on *Antichrist in the Apocalypse.*

William Burgh has given us the first systematic treatment of prophetic events following the new futurist interpretation in *Lectures on the Second Advent of Our Lord Jesus Christ* (1835). In 1820, Burgh had published a tract in which he followed the historical premillennial view, but he became converted to the new futurist interpretation.

Burgh knows of only one coming of Christ, at the end of the Tribulation when the dead in Christ will be raised and the living believers raptured. He believed that Israel was to be restored at the end of the age when the seventieth week of Daniel 9 would occur. Antichrist will make a covenant with Israel only to break it in the midst of the week and to turn in wrath against Israel. The second coming of Christ will bring destruction to Antichrist and a great outpouring of the Spirit upon Israel who will then become the center of the millennial kingdom to preach the Gospel of grace and to be the agency in the salvation of the Gentile nations. Christianity will then be extended without hindrance throughout the earth and the Gentiles will be brought *en masse* into the Church. The first resurrection at the beginning of the millennium will not include all the Church, for the greater part of the Church will come to salvation during the millennium. The first resurrection of saints to reign with Christ will be a blessing granted to those who have been willing to share Christ's sufferings and humiliation during this present evil age and especially in the time of Tribulation at the hands of Antichrist.

These early futurists followed a pattern of prophetic events similar to that found in the early fathers, with the necessary exception that Rome was not the final kingdom. In fact they appeal to the fathers against the popular historical interpretation for support of their basic view. A pretribulation rapture is utterly unknown by these men, and while Israel is to be restored, the Gospel which Israel will preach in the millennium is the Gospel of grace, and those who are saved are included in the Church. The Tribulation concerns both Israel and the Church; in fact, it will be the time of testing an apostate Christianity.

The Rise of Pretribulationism

A second out-growth of the prophetic awakening of the early nineteenth century was Darbyism, or Dispensationalism, which had its birth within the Plymouth Brethren movement. A pretribulation rapture is an essential element of this system. The Brethren movement had its beginnings in Dublin in 1825 when a small group of earnest men, dissatisfied with the spiritual condition of the Protestant church in Ireland, met for prayer and fellowship. Soon others joined the fellowship and other similar groups sprang up. In 1827, J. N. Darby entered the fellowship. Although there was an interest from the start in prophetic truth, the center of emphasis was "The Nature and Unity of the Church of Christ" (the title of Darby's first tract) in reaction to the deadness and formalism of the organized church and the ordained ministry. Outstanding among the new groups which arose in Ireland and England was the fellowship in Plymouth, from which the movement derived its name. Leader of the Plymouth fellowship for many years was B. W. Newton, a man of considerable learning and scholarship. Two other outstanding Brethren were S. P. Tregelles, recognized by the entire world of Biblical scholarship for his contribution to the study of the history of the Greek text of the New Testament, and George Muller, the great man of prayer.

We have already mentioned the Albury Park conference and the Powerscourt meetings. Darby and other leaders of the new movement attended the meetings at Powerscourt, and Darby's leadership in the area of prophetic interpretation here became evident. It was at Powerscourt that the teaching of a pretribulation rapture of the Church took shape. Tregelles, a member of the Brethren in these early days, tells us that the idea of a secret rapture at a secret coming of Christ had its origin in an "utterance" in Edward Irving's church, and that this was taken to be the voice of the Spirit. Tregelles says, "It was from that supposed revelation that the modern doctrine and the modern phraseology respecting it arose. It came not from Holy Scripture, but from that which falsely pretended to be the Spirit of God."[2] This doctrine together with other important modifications of the traditional futuristic view were vigorously promoted by Darby, and they have been popularized by the writings of William Kelly.

Not all of the Brethren accepted the teaching of a pretribulation rapture. In 1842, B. W. Newton of Plymouth published a book entitled *Thoughts on the Apocalypse*[3] in which he taught the traditional view that the Church would go through the Tribulation. There arose a sharp contention over the issue of pretribulationism between the two men. Newton "considered Mr. Darby's dispensational teaching as the height of speculative nonsense" (H. A. Ironside). He was supported in his posttribulation views by Tregelles.[4] A rift followed which was never healed. This was the first of a series of many contentions which marred the history of the Brethren movement.

Within early Brethrenism, we find two types of prophetic interpretation: the traditional futurism, and Darbyism or Dispensationalism. The influence which has extended to prophetic study in America has been the latter. Doubtless Newton's views on the Church and the Tribulation were discredited because he was accused of holding unsound views on the person of Christ.

Pretribulationism in America

In the early nineteenth century, postmillennialism was the prevailing interpretation of prophecy in America. Jon-

2. S. P. Tregelles, *The Hope of Christ's Second Coming*, first published in 1864, and now available at Ambassadors for Christ, Los Angeles, California.

3. This can be procured from The Sovereign Grace Advent Testimony, 9 Milnthorpe Rd., Chiswick, London, England.

4. See the book named above.

athan Edwards had accepted Whitbyan postmillennialism, and the publication of several popular commentaries widely disseminated the doctrine. Matthew Henry's famous commentary was published in America in 1828-29, and we are told that more than two hundred thousand volumes circulated by 1840. Henry applied the prophecies on Antichrist to the Papacy, and interpreted the first resurrection and the millennium to mean political restoration of those who had suffered at the hands of papal Rome. He understood the second resurrection to be the revival of political power of wicked men.

Thomas Scott's commentary, the most popular and widely quoted of the early nineteenth century works of its sort, spread the Whitbyan theory. Adam Clarke's commentary was first published in America in 1811-25. Clarke saw in Daniel's vision of the stone crushing the image a prophecy of the victory of the Church over the Roman empire, a victory which would extend until the Church filled the earth. Two of the most effective agencies in accomplishing this end were the British and Foreign Bible Society and the contemporary missionary enterprise. Clarke interpreted the second coming of Christ in Matthew 24 of the destruction of Jerusalem by Rome, and he understood the "end of the age" in Matthew 24:3,14 to refer to the end of the Jewish age accomplished at that time.

A reaction to postmillennialism arose in America as it had in England. This may be illustrated by two prophetic magazines. *The Literalist* was published in Philadelphia between 1840-1842 advocating, as its name indicates, a literal view of prophetic interpretation in opposition to the spiritualizing method of the predominant Whitbyism. *The American Millenarian and Prophetic Review* appeared in New York in the years 1842-44 with a similar objective. Both journals drew heavily upon writers of the English prophetic awakening such as Bickersteth, Brooks, and Cuninghame. In fact, the *Literalist* consisted largely of English reprints. Both journals followed the path marked out by their English exemplars of the historical "Protestant" interpretation with its 1260 years and papal Antichrist. Thus although thoroughly millenarian, they were not futurist in their understanding of the Tribulation and the Antichrist.

Against this background of prevailing postmillennialism and a groping search for a more satisfying interpretation of prophecy, it is easy to see how Darbyan futurism possessed such attraction and impelling power. It came with a freshness and vitality which quite captured American Christians. Darby visited America six times between 1859 and 1874 and was warmly welcomed. His system of prophetic interpretation was eagerly adopted, not because of the attractiveness of the details of his system, but because its basic futurism seemed to be a recovery of a sound Biblical prophetic interpretation — which in fact it was — and to give to the doctrine of the Lord's return the importance it deserved. In other words, Darbyism to many Christians meant the rediscovery of the precious Biblical truth of Christ's glorious second coming, even though the basic truth was accompanied by some important details which were not essential to the premillennial return of Christ and which many later came to feel were not in the Word of God. Once more, as in the early church, the return of Christ became a living and vital expectation in the lives of Christian people and in the pulpit ministry of many a preacher. Little wonder that the view has been cherished and defended with such deep emotional overtones. Darbyism in fact restored something precious which had long been lost.

This new prophetic emphasis at once found expression in the prophetic and Bible conference movement. A. C. Gaebelein, telling the story of the Scofield Reference Bible, finds its background within this movement. Interest in premillennialism grew to a point where a great prophetic conference was suggested by Nathaniel West. A call was issued by a committee of eight men, among whom were

James H. Brookes and A. J. Gordon, with the indorsement of one hundred and fourteen "Bishops, Professors, Ministers and Brethren." The conference was called to meet in the church of the Holy Trinity (Episcopal) in 1878. [5] A second prophetic conference was held in Chicago in 1886. [6] Prominent in these conferences were such men as Stephen Tyng, W. R. Nicholson, Nathaniel West, S. H. Kellogg, A. J. Gordon, James H. Brookes, W. J. Erdman, W. G. Moorehead and A. T. Pierson.

Another series of meetings of even greater importance was that which met at Niagara on Lake Ontario from 1883-1897. This conference was the outgrowth of a small Bible study fellowship initiated in 1875 by a handful of men among whom were Nathaniel West, J. H. Brookes and W. J. Erdman. They were joined the next year by A. J. Gordon. This group met from place to place until the conference at Ontario was undertaken. Among the leading teachers of the Ontario conferences, according to A. C. Gaebelein, were James H. Brookes, A. J. Gordon, W. J. Erdman, Albert Erdman, George C. Needham, A. C. Dickson, L. W. Mundhall, H. M. Parsons, Canon Howitt, E. P. Marvin, Hudson Taylor, J. M. Stifler, Robert Cameron, W. G. Moorehead and A. T. Pierson. After this pioneer of American Bible conferences was discontinued, a new conference at Seacliff, Long Island, was opened in 1901, and it was here that the plan for the Reference Bible embodying the dispensational system of interpretation occurred to Dr. C. I. Scofield.

In view of the modern notion that pretribulationism has been one of the foundational tenets of a sound presentation of prophetic truth, it is important to note that many of the leaders of this early prophetic, Bible conference movement either were or became posttribulationists. Many of the teachers at the Niagara Conference accepted J. N. Darby's

---

5. The addresses were published in *Premillennial Essays*, edited by Nathaniel West.
6. *Prophetic Studies of the International Prophetic Conference.*

pretribulation rapture along with the doctrine of Christ's return. Of the men named above, James H. Brookes, A. T. Pierson, and C. I. Scofield have been among the most influential supporters of this view. However, other teachers did not accept it, and still others accepted it at first only to give it up after more mature study of the Word of God. Since it is often thought that all good and godly premillennialists must be pretribulationists, we shall note the views of several of these leaders who did not adhere to the pretribulation teaching.

Nathaniel West suggested and arranged the first prophetic conference in 1878 and was one of the leading teachers. His book, *The Thousand Years in Both Testaments* (1880), has been called the most important defense of premillennialism which has been written. However, West had no patience with pretribulationism. He taught that the 144,000 who are sealed in Revelation 7 are the fulfillment of the promise in Romans 11 — the salvation of literal Israel. Their salvation will occur at the beginning of the seventieth week as a result of the ministry of the two witnesses (Rev. 11), and they are sealed that they might take the place of the Church which is seen in the great multitude in Revelation 7 — a multitude which is to suffer near extinction at the hands of Antichrist in the Great Tribulation. "They (these two groups) assure us also that the Christian Church will not be removed from the earth, or become extinct under persecution, but, reduced and suffering, will also live to see the Advent" (p. 245). "They (the 144,000) are . . . the Israelitish Church of the Future . . . . It is not that Gentile believers have utterly perished in the apostasy, for Paul teaches the contrary. I Thess. iv:16,17; nor that no Jewish believers become martyrs, for John teaches otherwise, Rev. vii:9 . . . . But it is that, in the height of the apostasy, when the true Church is almost gone, God will restore Israel, and preserve of Israel an election, undestroyed by the tribulation, who shall live to see the Advent" (p. 249). West believed not that the Church would be removed by rapture and its place taken by a Jewish remnant, but that the Church would be removed by persecution and martyrdom.

These views were published in 1880 when emphasis upon pretribulationism had not yet become strong. In a later book (*Daniel's Great Prophecy*, 1898) when the issue had become more important and pretribulationism had won many supporters, West expressed himself in far more vigorous terms. Speaking of the 70th week, he said, "All the devices of interpretation which torture the Word of God to support a vain theory of exemption of the church from the tribulation are forever shattered" (p. 128). "It is needless to say that the apostles followed their Master's teaching, and took his Olivet discourse as the textbook of their eschatology. It ruled the whole faith of the early church. It settled every heresy as to the time of the advent. It corrected the Thessalonian error as to the 'any moment view.' Paul appeals to it to decide the question" (p. 130). "When the Antichrist and the Jews are in covenant, at the beginning of the 70th week, and clearer still, when the breach occurs between them at the middle of the week, then the determination of the year, perhaps the month, but never the day or hour will be certain, i.e., to all believers" (p. 131). Is pretribulationism a device which tortures the Word of God? a vain theory? a heresy? an error? So West believed.

A. J. Gordon

Another great man of God and student of the prophetic Word was A. J. Gordon, famed pastor of Clarendon Street Baptist Church in Boston, where he experienced many movings of the Spirit of God in revival. Gordon joined the Bible study fellowship in its second year and was a constant speaker at the Niagara conference. Yet if he were alive today, many zealous brethren would be ready to pronounce him dangerous.

In his book on the Lord's coming (*Ecce Venit*, 1889), Gordon parts company with the whole Darby system of interpretation. Although he constantly emphasized the importance of the truth of the Lord's return and often sounds like one who holds the "any-moment" view, Gordon did not look for a personal Antichrist and a three and a half year Tribulation. In its stead, he embraced the historical interpretation believing it is "more scriptural, and rests upon the more obvious and simple interpretation of the Word" (p. vi). Antichrist was the Papacy; the temple of God in which Antichrist sits in II Thessalonians 2 was the Church. "Where a Judaizing interpretation would lead us from this phrase of the apostle, to imagine a future temple rebuilt in Jerusalem, enthroning an infidel Antichrist, we have only to collate the passages in which the expression occurs to find how invariably it stands for Christ's mystical body, the church" (pp. 110f).

What then of the three and a half years of Antichrist's reign? Adopting the usual day-year theory of the historical school, Gordon believed that by the use of the 1260 years, "If the rise of the papacy could be fixed as to the exact day and year, we might not err in seeking by computation for the day and year of its fall, and so approximate closely the date of the coming of the Lord" (p. 205). Where does this leave the usual "any-moment" theory which holds that Christ could have returned at any moment after His ascension? How could the coming of Christ have been "imminent" to anyone living before the 1260 years had elapsed?

As to the details of Christ's return, Gordon said, "Will He be visible to His Church alone at His Parousia, manifesting Himself unto them, but not to the world until a later epiphany, when He shall appear in glory with His saints? Already there has been too much dogmatizing on these points; therefore we prefer to leave them for the day to reveal" (p. 211). On the secret rapture, he said, "upon the whole question of a secret rapture, we would speak with reserve, knowing that there are scriptures which give a different impression" (p. 246). There is no hint in Gordon's book of anything but a single, glorious, visible coming of Christ.

W. J. Erdman

One of the key men in the movement was W. J. Erdman, who served as secretary and leader of the Niagara Bible Conference for more than twenty years, and who also was one of the consulting editors of the Scofield Reference Bible. In his story of the Scofield Bible, A. C. Gaebelein describes Erdman as "an able, logical, and spiritual teacher of the Word." Dr. Erdman was pastor of the Moody Church in Chicago when Darby visited that city and at first he accepted Darby's pretribulation, any-moment view of Christ's return. Upon further searching of the Scriptures, Erdman decided that this view was not taught in the Word, and he felt he could no longer support a view for which he could not find Scriptural warrant. He thereupon wrote a tract entitled, "A Theory Reviewed" in which he questioned the any-moment theory, concluding with these words: "Should any deplore the adoption of the belief that the Lord will not come any moment, as if it would take away all joy and comfort, it is enough to answer in the words of another, 'Better the disappointment of truth than the fair but false promises of error.' " Erdman continued to believe in Christ's premillennial coming and that His return might take place within his own generation. However, he believed that the Church must pass through the Tribulation. In his *Notes on the Revelation*, Erdman said of the saints who are to be persecuted by Antichrist, "unless the contrary can be proved, it is a fair inference from many facts that by the 'saints' seen as future by Daniel and by John are meant 'the Church' which consists of Jews and Gentiles" (p. 47).

Robert Cameron

Another teacher, coming into the fellowship in 1878, was Robert Cameron. He like Erdman at first accepted the Darby teaching but later turned from it. In 1922, he wrote *Scriptural Truth About the Lord's Return* in which he set forth his mature conclusions. "The *Coming for* and the *Coming with*, the saints, still persists, although it involves a manifest contradiction, viz., *two* Second Comings which is an absurdity" (p. 16). "Everywhere in the New Testament it is taught that to suffer for Christ is one of the highest honors Christians can have bestowed upon them. A desire to shirk suffering for Christ is a sign of degeneracy. At the close of this dispensation, it will still be counted an honor to suffer shame for our adorable Lord" (p. 18). The entire book is devoted to a refutation of the any-moment theory of Christ's coming.

Henry W. Frost

In 1885, Henry W. Frost attended the Niagara Conference for the first time and there received his first impulse toward missionary service, an impulse which blossomed in a ministry of thirty-six years of service for the China Inland Mission as Home Director. Frost also served as recording secretary for the Niagara conference.

In 1924, Frost wrote *Matthew Twenty-four and the Revelation,* and from it we would extract one passage. Frost discusses interpretations of Matthew 24 which he believes to be unscriptural. One such view is that "Christ taught that the saints, dead and living, would be caught up to meet Him in the air at His coming, that this coming would occur before the seven-year-rule of the Antichrist, that during the tribulation of the following seven years many persecuted ones would be converted, that these would form a last band of Christians, and then, that these too, dead and living, would be caught up to meet the Lord in the air as He descends to the earth with those saints who were previously resurrected and translated." This view, says Frost, "might be held as truth if there were any scripture to confirm it, but (it) may not be held in view of the fact that no scripture even suggests such a process of events and many scriptures positively contradict it . . . . Nowhere do the Epistles state that the coming will take place before the tribulation, most passages being silent as to the time and some passages strongly teaching a post-tribulation advent." Frost's conclusion is that "living Christians will go into and through the tribulation" (p. 69).

W. G. Moorehead

The name of W. G. Moorehead of Xenia Theological Seminary from 1873 to 1914, appears in the call for the first prophetic conference in 1878. He was active in the Niagara movement from 1882; and his name will be found in the Scofield Reference Bible as a consulting editor. Yet he has written, "What becomes of (the saints) and of the Lord whom they encounter in the air (at the Rapture)? Do they abide there? No, their stay in the air is but brief, — momentary. There are only two other places in the New Testament where the phrase 'to meet' occurs . . . and in both of them the party met continues to advance still in the direction in which he was moving previously. Augustine perceived this: 'It is as He is coming, not abiding, that we shall go to meet Him.' Christ does not return to heaven with His saints; He comes on with them to the earth. As an ancient writer expresses it, — 'We shall be caught away to meet Christ, that all may come with the Lord to battle.'" Here is a clear rejection by an editor of the Scofield Bible of the pretribulation rapture of the Church with the two comings of Christ which is found in the Scofield Bible.

Charles R. Erdman

Among the scholars who contributed to the formation of the Scofield Reference Bible was Dr. C. R. Erdman of Princeton. In the Introduction of the Reference Bible, Scofield includes him among those "learned and spiritual brethren in Europe and America to whose labours he is indebted for suggestions of inestimable value."

Yet Erdman did not follow the prophetic outline taught by Scofield. Referring to the idea of a secret, any-moment rapture before the Tribulation with its two comings of Christ, Erdman says, "The doctrine appears to be founded upon a false interpretation of the translation, in the King James Version, of the opening verse of the second chapter of Second Thessalonians. . . . The Revised Version, however, directly contradicts this mistaken view . . . He (Paul) clearly stated that the day in which believers were to be delivered from their tribulations, the day of Christ's coming and of their 'gathering together unto him,' would not dawn 'except the falling away' came first and 'the Man of Sin' was revealed" (*The Return of Christ,* pp. 54f).

How are we to account for the fact that a view which was at first quite widely accepted was later given up by so many of the outstanding leaders of the prophetic and Bible conference movement? Was it because of pernicious influences which turned them away from the pure teaching of the Word of God? Was it due to enemies of pretribulationism who prevailed upon these leaders to abandon the truth? Was it due to inroads of liberalism? None of these suggestions gives us the correct answer, which appears to rest in a simple historical fact. At the beginnings of the movement, the premillennialism which was so warmly received and taught was the Darby type of premillennialism with its pretribulation rapture. The two doctrines were thought by most of the teachers to be synonymous; but the emphasis was placed on the Lord's return, not on such details as the relationship of the Rapture to the Tribulation. Pretribulationism was accepted "uncritically" along with a sound premillennialism. The thrust of James H. Brookes' influential book *Maranatha* (1878) shows that the enemy of that day was postmillennialism. Pretribulationism or posttribulationism were not issues. The Darby view of a pretribulation rapture was accepted without much question or careful study.

However, some of the outstanding teachers were unable to go along with the pretribulation theory, among them Nathaniel West and A. J. Gordon. Later in the movement, when greater emphasis began to be laid upon the details, the teachers began to study the Word more carefully, and many of them came to realize that along with sound Biblical premillennialism, they had accepted a teaching which upon mature reflection and study they decided was not Biblical. They had the courage publicly to reverse themselves at this point without in any way giving up the essentials of a Biblical doctrine of the Lord's premillennial return.

Throughout the entire movement as we have traced it, pretribulationism was never a teaching which was considered essential to a sound, Biblical view of The Blessed Hope. Men who differed at these points were not accused of betraying the Bible. In more recent times, due to the influence of the Scofield Reference Bible, the Bible school movement, etc., pretribulationism has been more widely accepted than ever before with the result that many Christians have never heard any sound Bible teachers who held a different position and therefore have naturally concluded that pretribulationism is *essential* to premillenialism. This is not true historically, and it is not true theologically or Biblically.

The teachers of the Word whose views we have discussed were all associated with the prophetic and Bible conference movement of a half century ago when pretribulationism was taking root in American Christian thought. We must add the views of others of more recent date who are outstanding men of God and defenders of the faith, who have found themselves compelled to abandon pretribulationism.

Philip Mauro was a patent lawyer who, after conversion, gave himself vigorously to the defense of the faith. He is included among the writers of the *Fundamentals* and produced some twenty-five books.

Mauro at first espoused dispensationalism. In 1913 he wrote *Looking For the Saviour* in which he defended the usual pretribulation rapture of the Church. In *The Kingdom of Heaven* (1918) he departed from the dispensational view of the postponed kingdom but was still a premillenarian. In *The Patmos Visions, A Study of the Apocalypse* (1925) he forsook the usual futurist interpretation of the Revelation, seeing in the two beasts the Roman empire and the Papacy. Finally, in *The Gospel of the Kingdom* (1928), Mauro broke completely with dispensationalism. Among the reasons was the sudden realization that the Scofield Bible "has usurped the place of authority that belongs to God's Bible alone." He says further, "It is mortifying to remember that I not only held and taught these novelties myself, but that I even enjoyed a complacent sense of superiority because thereof, and regarded with feelings of pity and contempt those who had not received the 'new light' and were unacquainted with this up-to-date method of 'rightly dividing the word of truth.' . . . The time came . . . . when the inconsistencies and self-contradictions of the system itself, and above all, the impossibility of reconciling its main positions with the plain statement of the Word of God, became so glaringly evident that I could not do otherwise than to renounce it."

Rowland V. Bingham was General Director of the Sudan Interior Mission, President of Canadian Keswick Conference, and Editor of *The Evangelical Christian*. In 1937, Bingham published a little book under the title, *Matthew The Publican and His Gospel* in which he set forth his changed views. In the Introduction, he tells us that during the first period of his Christian life he accepted the Gospel of Matthew at face value and revelled in its truth. But later he came in contact with dispensational writings which for the first time presented to his mind the reality of the second coming of Christ. "Never having listened to a single address on the Second Coming of Christ, I at once became infatuated with prophetic study." The second period of his life thus was dominated by a dispensational interpretation. "The reiteration of these (dispensational) propositions by such great and godly men whose names are known and beloved by the whole Church, many of them personally known and loved by me, had made their impression upon me."

There came a day, however, when his wife asked him, "Rowland, where do you get the 'Secret Rapture' idea in the Bible?" Bingham had no satisfactory answer; and he was driven to study the Word of God afresh but in deep confusion. Finally, faced with a week's Bible conference but with no message, "in sheer desperation I took out my Bible and threw myself helplessly on the Lord. And I know the blessed Illuminator, the Holy Spirit, responded. I commenced to read in Matthew, and all day long I read and reread, with such an unveiling that my soul was filled to . . . overflowing. . . My old theories were being dispelled like mists before the sunshine. It means a great deal to have the cherished teaching of years upset in a day, and that without argument or human instrument." After outlining the interpretation to which he was driven, he adds, "As time has gone by, all my future study has confirmed me in the changed views of that day. In the study of this book I cannot expect to carry with me all those whose cherished teaching of years it upsets. I simply in the whole prophetic sphere plead for that liberty of interpretation which I gladly accord to others."

G. Campbell Morgan was one of the most gifted Bible teachers and expositors of the Word of God of the preceding generation. It is difficult indeed to discover Dr. Morgan's position in matters of prophetic interpretation, for different writings suggest different viewpoints. Sometimes he writes as though he were a thorough-going dispensationalist. In an early book (*God's Methods with Man*, 1898) Morgan distinguished between the Gospel of the Kingdom and the Gospel of Paul and offered the usual dispensational outline of prophetic events (p. 172). In *The*

Teaching of Christ (1913), he devoted a third of the book to our Lord's teaching about the Kingdom of God, but no dispensationalism is to be found. Almost no reference is made to Israel's relation to the Kingdom. Rather, the Kingdom is primarily the rule of God, then the sphere in which the rule is realized, and finally the results of that rule. The Kingdom is to be established by processes leading to, and culminating in a crisis — the second coming of Christ. Speaking of the Olivet Discourse, he says that the Church is the instrument of the Kingdom in the economy of God. In this book, Morgan sounds more like an amillennialist than a dispensationalist.

How can we account for these two points of view? We can only conclude that Morgan changed his interpretation of prophetic truth. Perhaps Philip Mauro's writings contributed to the change. We quoted at some length from Mauro's *The Gospel of the Kingdom*. Of the argument of this book, Morgan wrote, "It is unanswerable." Furthermore, Morgan reviewed Mauro's *Study of the Apocalypse* which departs radically from the usual futurist interpretation and wrote, "(My) reading results in a conviction that the general thesis is completely established. It is the most lucid and satisfying work on the Apocalypse that I have ever read."

Nor is this all. When Rowland Bingham's *Matthew the Publican* appeared, Morgan wrote to Bingham in the following words: "I suppose I may say that across the years I have passed through very much of your own experience with regard to these prophetic matters. At any rate, at the moment I accept without any qualification the philosophy of your interpretation . . . . I think the view that makes Matthew Jewish is utterly false. The phrase 'secret Rapture' has to me for a long time been a very objectionable one, and utterly unwarranted in its wording, and in what it is made to stand for by the teaching of Scripture."

Bishop Frank Houghton, General Director of the China Inland Mission since 1940, has written, "While our primary emphasis must surely be upon the *fact* of our Lord's personal coming, and the obligation upon us who have this hope to 'purify ourselves, even as He is pure,' and to bear witness to His Gospel in all lands, I cannot but say that, as the years go by, I am more and more amazed that any one should claim to have found *in the Scriptures* justification for the view that the coming is to be in two stages (one secret and the other public), and that the Church will escape the Tribulation.

"We are on unsafe ground as soon as we begin to conjecture, apart from the clear statements of Scripture, what God is, or is not, likely to do."

Oswald J. Smith is known around the world because of his great zeal for world evangelization. We are compelled to conclude that Dr. Smith experienced a change of view about the Rapture and the Tribulation. In his book, *Is the Antichrist at Hand?* (1926) he wrote, "I have always held the view that the rapture precedes the revelation by some seven years, and that the Church therefore will not go through the Tribulation." He admits that he cannot be dogmatic and that his mind is open toward the other view.

Apparently his mind was shortly changed, for a year later appeared *When Antichrist Reigns* in which he sees the Church in the Tribulation. He holds that Matthew 24 is the seventieth week of Daniel. Verses 1-14 describe the first half of the week, and verses 15-51 the second half of the week. Of verses 9-10 which fall in the first half of the final seven year period, Smith says, "So the church will again be bitterly persecuted even to the point of martyrdom." Of the Great Tribulation and the appearance of Antichrist, he says, "For when the Antichrist emerges from the temple it will be to exterminate both Jews and Christians alike." False prophets will tell "the fleeing Christians and Jews that the Messiah has come and is at Jerusalem." Applying these truths, he writes, "Surely the hour is at hand. The great tribulation must be almost upon us, the fearful reign of the Antichrist about to commence. And then the battle of Armageddon, and then — the glorious revelation of our blessed Lord. And then, ah, then, at last, at last, the Golden Age, the Millennium. Hasten, glad Day! Hasten, judgment and tribulation! Hasten, oh hasten, Thou Christ of God, Thou mighty Prince of Peace!" He then describes the return of Christ which he finds in verse 31: "As He descends the trumpet sounds, and the angels are dispatched to gather the elect and to bear them in the twinkling of an eye to their Lord and Master." This apparently is the Rapture of the Church.

That this represents Dr. Smith's present views may be seen from the fact that this chapter was reprinted, with only minor verbal changes, in *Prophecy — What Lies Ahead?* (1952). In this book, Christ's return is placed after the Tribulation. If the question of the Rapture and Tribulation, Dr. Smith says, "But, you ask, is the Church to go through the Tribulation? That is not the question. It is this: Is the Church ready? Are you ready, ready either for Tribulation or Rapture? If you are, that is all that matters. What difference does it make so long as you are ready? . . . If you are to be in it, you cannot escape, and, if you are to escape, you will not be in it." This is hardly the language of pretribulationism.

Dr. Harold John Ockenga, Pastor of Park Street Church, Boston, has been raised up by the Lord to be one of the giants of our day in defending the faith, in the winning of souls through the promotion of evangelism in New England and through evangelistic campaigns, and in the prosecution of worldwide evangelization. When he came to his present church, the missionary budget was less than $2500. After nineteen years this has been raised to $220,000.

Writing in *Christian Life* (February, 1955), Dr. Ockenga tells us how he came to give up his pretribulation eschatology and to believe that the Church would enter into the Great Tribulation. The article is very brief and is more a personal testimony than a defense of posttribulationism. Insuperable difficulties were recognized in pretribulationism. "Is it conceivable that the Jews without the Pentecostal presence and power of the Holy Spirit will do during the tribulation what the church in Holy Spirit power could not do in 2,000 years?" "No amount of explaining can make (I Thess. 4:16,17) a secret rapture. It is the visible accompaniment of the glorious advent of the Lord. No exegetical justification exists for the arbitrary separation of the 'coming of Christ' and the 'day of the Lord.' It is one 'day of the Lord Jesus Christ.'" "Another shattering blow to my dispensational eschatology came when I realized that the church age is not a parenthesis in the divine redemptive plan but is the great era of redemption, of salvation, and of revival."

These men, like those of the earlier generation, passed through the experience of accepting dispensational teaching but of being driven to conclude that it did not coincide with the teachings of the Word of God. But who is to say that Mauro, Bingham, Morgan, Houghton, Smith and Ockenga are any less men of God and true to the Word? The author is personally acquainted with other Christian leaders who have given up pretribulationism; but they have not gone on record and so cannot be quoted.

Pretribulationism has not been and never ought to be a test of a sound view of prophetic truth. Pretribulationism is a recent view which was formulated 125 years ago by one wing of the Plymouth Brethren and accepted in America by a circle of devout and godly men but rejected by others who were equally devout and godly and equally devoted to the propagation of the truth of the Lord's return.

There ought to be today liberty in the interpretation of the Word at this point. It is a reversal of history and Scripturally indefensible to label any deviation from a pretribulation eschatology a step toward liberalism, and it is holding up a human interpretation as though it had the authority of Scripture itself.

One of America's outstanding pretribulationists was H. A Ironside; we would do well to imitate his words of charity toward those who differed with him. Speaking of Baptist theologian A. H. Strong's accusation of heresy in Brethren doctrine, Ironside replied, "It passes our comprehension how any man, or set of men, with an atom of genuine love for the Lord and His people, can deliberately brand as heretics fellow-believers whose lives are generally fragrant with Christian graces, who stand unflinchingly for the inspiration of the entire Bible, simply because they hold different views on prophecy. Dr. Strong evidently does *not* believe in the secret rapture of the saints, but in the coming of the Lord in judgment at the end of the world. 'Brethren' would not brand him as a heretic for this, though they feel he has lost much by his defective views." Let us distinguish if we will between adequate and defective views of prophetic interpretation, but let us not be guilty of accusing another of heresy or liberalism because he does not agree with our pattern of prophetic truth.

Those who "love His appearing" should close ranks and stand together on the great fundamentals of the Word of God. A monument to American Fundamentalism is the series of twelve small volumes, published in 1909-11, financed by two laymen and sent to every Protestant minister in America. The purpose of *The Fundamentals* was to unite those who stood squarely on the fundamentals of the faith and to make a powerful statement in face of the inroads of liberalism. Included in the circle of defenders of the faith were not only dispensationalists like R. A. Torrey, A. T. Pierson, J. M. Gray, C. I. Scofield and A. C. Gaebelein, but non-dispensationalists like W. G. Moorehead, W. J. Erdman, H. W. Frost and C. R. Erdman, and even postmillennialists James Orr, B. B. Warfield, and E. Y. Mullins. Why can such unity not be demonstrated today?

Ten years later, the Fundamentalist movement within the Northern Baptist Convention was organized. Describing the first Fundamentalist convention held in Buffalo in 1920, Curtis Lee Laws wrote, "The movement . . . was in no sense a premillennialist movement, but in every sense a conservative movement. Premillennialists were much in evidence because premillennialists are always sound on the fundamentals, but eschatological questions did not enter into any of the Buffalo controversies. Standing solidly together in the battle for the re-enthronement of the fundamentals of our holy faith were premillennialists, postmillennialists, promillennialists and nomillennialists. Fortunately the conservative group contains no one who repudiates the blessed doctrine of the second coming of our Lord, but the group does contain those who differ radically with one another concerning the whole millennial question." If those who are "set for the defense of the faith" can stand together in the same spirit of basic unity in spite of differences in details, they will win far more ground than they will if they squander their energies in controversy.

3

THE VOCABULARY OF THE BLESSED HOPE

IN THE first two chapters, we have traced the history of prophetic interpretation and discovered three things. The Blessed Hope of the early church was not a pretribulation rapture but the second coming of Christ at the end of the Tribulation. Pretribulationism is a teaching which arose in the nineteenth century among the Plymouth Brethren whence it came to America where, for historical reasons which can be discerned, it was warmly received and widely propagated. However, many devout men who first accepted this teaching were later, upon mature study, compelled to reverse themselves and admit that they could not find this doctrine in the Word of God.

We must now look more closely into the Scriptures to discover what they teach concerning the return of Christ, the Rapture and the Tribulation, and we would first look at the vocabulary which is used of Christ's second advent. Strictly speaking, the Bible has little to say about a "second advent." Hebrews 9:28 says that he "shall appear a second time," and Acts 1:11 reads, "this Jesus, who was received up from you into heaven, shall so come in like manner as ye beheld him going into heaven."[1] The expression, "the second advent" is the language of theology; the expression does not occur in Scripture. The Word speaks of His coming (*parousia*), His revelation (*apokalypsis*) and His manifestation (*epiphaneia*).

Pretribulationism teaches that the second coming of Christ is to be divided into two aspects which, it is assumed,

---

1. Scriptural quotations are from the American Version of 1901. Occasionally, the author has varied the translation in the interests of closer conformity to the Greek.

are separated by the Great Tribulation. These two events are called the Rapture and the Revelation. The Rapture, or catching up of the Church to meet the Lord in the air, is a different event from the Revelation when He will appear in the manifestation of His glory. The Rapture occurs before the Tribulation, while the Revelation occurs when Christ comes to end the Tribulation and to execute righteous judgment upon the earth. At the Rapture, Christ comes in the air *for* His saints (Jn. 14:3); during the interval of the seven year Tribulation, the saints are with the Lord in the air receiving their rewards at the *bema* of Christ. At the Revelation, Christ comes to earth *with* His saints (I Thess. 3:13). As one writer has said, "He certainly must come for them before he can come with them."

Since the Rapture precedes the Tribulation, it is assumed that it may occur at any moment; but the Revelation cannot occur until after the appearance of Antichrist and the Great Tribulation. "The failure to make this distinction has led to great confusion among commentators on this subject." The coming of Christ for the Rapture of the Church will be a secret coming and will be invisible to any except the Church; while the Revelation will be a glorious outshining which will be evident to all the world.

Such is the outline of prophetic events taught by pretribulationists. Is this view really taught in the Word of God? If such a pattern of truth is really embodied in the Scriptures, it should be evident from an analysis of the terminology which is used in connection with the coming of Christ. If however this terminology does not sustain the teaching of two aspects in Christ's coming, we shall be forced to conclude that His return will be a single, glorious event.

Parousia. Three words are employed in the New Testament to describe the second advent. The first is parousia which means "coming," "arrival" or "presence." This is His people glory and honor because of their steadfastness is used in connection with the Rapture of the Church. "We that are alive, that are left unto the parousia of the Lord, shall in no wise precede them that are fallen asleep. For the Lord himself shall descend from heaven, with a shout, with the voice of the archangel, and with the trump of God; and the dead in Christ shall rise first: then we that are alive, that are left, shall together with them be caught up in the clouds to meet the Lord in the air; and so shall we ever be with the Lord" (I Thess. 4:15-17). It is very difficult to find a secret coming of Christ in these verses. His coming will be attended with a shout, with the voice of the archangel, and with the heavenly trumpet. Someone has said that the shout and the trumpet sound will be loud enough to wake the dead!

Furthermore, the parousia of Christ will occur not only to rapture the Church and to raise the righteous dead, but also to destroy the Man of Lawlessness, the Antichrist. "And then shall be revealed the lawless one, whom the Lord Jesus shall slay with the breath of his mouth, and bring to naught by the manifestation of his parousia" (II Thess. 2:8). This is obviously no secret event, for the parousia of Christ will be an outshining, a manifestation. Furthermore, this verse locates the parousia at the end of the Tribulation. One would naturally conclude by comparing the verses just cited that the Rapture of the living saints, the resurrection of those who have died, and the judgment upon the Antichrist will all take place at the same time, namely, at the parousia of Jesus at the end of Tribulation.

Furthermore, it is at His parousia that Jesus will be accompanied by all His saints. Paul prays that God may establish the Thessalonians in holiness "at the parousia of our Lord Jesus with all his saints" (I Thess. 3:13). At His parousia the Lord will come to bring His saints with Him, to raise the righteous dead, to rapture the living believers, and to destroy Antichrist.

The parousia will be a glorious event. Christ will destroy the Man of Lawlessness by the breath of his mouth and "by the manifestation (literally, "epiphany" or "out-shining") of his parousia" (II Thess. 2:8). The rendition of the King James version is not wrong: "by the bright-ness of his coming." This epiphany will be a glorious event, for Paul speaks of "the epiphany of the glory of our great God and our Saviour" (Titus 2:13).

We find the same teaching of a glorious visible parousia in Jesus' words. "For as the lightning cometh forth from the east, and is seen even unto the west; so shall be the parousia of the Son of man" (Matt. 24:27). It will be like a bolt of lightning, glorious, visible, evident to all.

The usual answer given to these facts by those who sep-arate the coming of Christ into two parts is that parousia means "presence" and therefore covers the entire period of time which is introduced by the Rapture and the beginning of the Tribulation. Thus, we are told, parousia can refer either to the coming of Christ at the Rapture or to His Revelation at the end of the Tribulation.

It is true that sometimes parousia does mean "presence." Paul contrasts his presence (parousia) with the Philip-pians with his absence (*apousia*) from them (Phil. 2:12). The Corinthians accused Paul of inconsistency, because "his letters . . . are strong, but his bodily presence is weak" (II Cor. 10:10). However, the word does not always mean "presence"; more often it means "arrival." When Paul in Ephesus received envoys from Corinth, he rejoiced at their parousia, i.e., their coming or arrival (I Cor. 16:17). When Paul was concerned about the condition of things at Cor-inth, he was comforted by the arrival (parousia) of Titus (II Cor. 7:6). It was not the presence of Titus but his ar-rival with good news from Corinth that provided the com-fort. To translate parousia by "presence" would empty it of its particular point. This is illustrated in the following instances: "Be patient, brethren, until the parousia of the Lord . . . Be ye also patient; establish your hearts; for the parousia of the Lord is at hand" (Jas. 5:7-8). "Where is the promise of his parousia?" (II Pet. 3:4). In these verses it is the coming, the return, the advent of the Lord which is called for; "presence" does not suit the context.

It is not the "presence" so much as the "coming" of Christ which is required in the verses we have just discussed. It is at the coming, the advent of Christ, that the dead will be raised and the living caught up; "presence" does not fit. It is at His coming, His advent, not His presence, that He will be accompanied by His saints. His coming, His advent, will be like a bolt of lightning. The parousia of Christ is His second coming, and it will bring both salvation and judgment: salvation of the saints, and judgment of the world.

Apokalypse. A second word used of our Lord's return is *apokalypsis* which means "revelation." The apokalypse or Revelation of Christ is distinguished by pretribulationists from the Rapture of the Church and is placed at the end of the Tribulation when Christ comes in glory to bring judgment upon the world. If this view is correct, then *the apokalypse of Christ is not primarily The Blessed Hope of the Christian.* When the Revelation occurs, the saints will have been raptured and will have received from the hand of Christ their rewards for the things done in the body. They will already have entered into the full enjoyment of life and fellowship with Christ. The apokalypse of Christ is for judgment of the wicked, not for the salvation of the Church. According to pretribulationism, the Rapture at the secret coming of Christ is our blessed hope and the object of our fond expectation, not the Revelation.

This, however, is not what we find in the Scripture. We are *"waiting for* the revelation of our Lord Jesus Christ" (I Cor. 1:7). According to pretribulationism, we are not waiting for the Revelation but for the Rapture. The Church is to suffer affliction until the time of the apokalypse of Christ. Paul says that "it is a righteous thing with God to recompense affliction to them that afflict you, and to you that are afflicted, rest with us, at the revelation of the Lord Jesus Christ from heaven, with the angels of his power in

flaming fire" (II Thess. 1:6,7). According to pretribulationism, this rest from persecution has already been experienced at the Rapture; it does not await the Revelation
of Jesus Christ. But the Word of God says it is received at
the Revelation.

It has recently been argued that the expression in the
Greek does not mean "when the Lord Jesus shall be revealed," but "in the revelation of the Lord Jesus," i.e., not
the moment when Christ is revealed but the period of time
during which His revelation occurs. When Christ is revealed, the afflicted will already be enjoying rest.

This however is a very unnatural interpretation of Paul's
language. Let us take note of the full expression: "if indeed
it is a righteous thing with God to recompense . . . to you
who are afflicted rest with us, in the revelation of the Lord
Jesus." The verb "to recompense" controls two objects:
1. affliction to those who afflict you; 2. rest to you who are
afflicted. Both the recompense of affliction and of rest will
be "in the revelation of the Lord." If affliction is to be
given when Christ is revealed, then the rest must also be
given when Christ is revealed. To say that the rest has
already been received and is being enjoyed is imposing upon the verse an assumption which is controverted by the
wording of the passage.

Peter employs the same expression. Now we are par-
takers of the sufferings of Christ, that "at the revelation of
his glory also ye may rejoice with exceeding joy" (I Pet.
4:13). This suggests that the fiery trial will be terminated
only at the apokalypse of Christ. Furthermore, Peter says
that the genuineness of our faith will bring "praise and
glory and honor at the revelation of Jesus Christ" (I Pet.
1:7). According to pretribulationism, this glory and honor
has already been experienced at an earlier time at the Rapture of the Church. This verse, however, asserts that one
of the purposes of the apokalypse of Christ is to bring to
His people glory and honor because of their steadfastness
in their faith. Finally, Peter assures us that our hope of

the perfection in grace will be brought unto us at the Revelation of Jesus Christ (I Pet. 1:13). All of these promises direct our hope of the fullness of our salvation not to the Rapture but to the Revelation of Christ. If these two events are one and the same, these verses are full of meaning. If, however, these blessings are not received at the Revelation but at an earlier Rapture, these verses are quite perplexing and difficult. It is difficult to see how a distinction can be made between these two events. The Revelation is continually made the object of our hope; the Rapture must therefore occur at the Revelation of Christ. The Scripture nowhere asserts that there is a Rapture which will take place before the Revelation.

Epiphany. The third word which is used of Christ's second coming is *epiphaneia* which means "manifestation" and must therefore, according to the pretribulation scheme, refer not to the Rapture of the Church and a secret coming of Christ at the beginning of the Tribulation but to the Revelation of Christ with His saints at the end of the Tribulation to bring judgment upon the world. It is indeed used in this latter meaning, for Christ will slay the man of lawlessness by the "epiphany of his parousia" (II Thess. 2:8). It is clear that His epiphany will occur at the end of the Tribulation.

This epiphany of Christ is, however, like His apokalypse the object of the believer's hope, as it could not be if the Church had received the object of its hope at an earlier time at the Rapture. Paul exhorts us to keep the commandment without spot and without reproach "until the epiphany of our Lord Jesus Christ" (I Tim. 6:14). At the end of his life, Paul expresses confidence that he has fought a good fight, and looking forward to the day of rewards at the judgment seat of Christ, he says, "henceforth there is laid up for me a crown of righteousness which the Lord the righteous judge shall give me at that day; and not to me only, but also to all them that have loved his epiphany" (II Tim. 4:8). One can only conclude from a passage such as this that "that day" which Paul anticipates as a day of rewards is the day of Christ's epiphany. It is therefore a day upon which Christians have set their affection, the object of Christian hope. And it is the day of giving rewards to believers. Pretribulationism places the judgment of rewards *between* the Rapture and the Revelation. Here, it is located at the epiphany, which is the same as the Revelation, at the end of the Tribulation.

This line of thought is clinched by Titus 2:13 and 14: "looking for the blessed hope and the *epiphany* of the glory of the great God and Saviour Jesus Christ; who gave himself for us, that he might redeem us from all iniquity and purify unto himself a people for his own possession, zealous of good works." The Blessed Hope of the Church is the epiphany of the glory of our God and Savior Jesus Christ.

If the Rapture of the Church, when we are caught up to meet Christ in the air, is separated by a considerable period of time from His apokalypse and His epiphany, then this is strange language indeed. For according to pretribulationism the coming of Christ at the end of the Tribulation has nothing to do with the reward of His saints or with the salvation of the righteous. The dead have already been raised and the living translated into their resurrection bodies. The judgment of works is now past and the rewards of Christ to His faithful servants have been distributed. The apokalypse and the epiphany of Christ at the end of the Tribulation have as their object judgment and not salvation. *Yet according to the Word of God, this epiphany is our blessed hope;* it is the time when we shall be rewarded; it is the time when we shall be redeemed from all iniquity and purified to become God's perfect possession; it is the Blessed Hope of perfect union in fellowship with Christ. Does it not seem then that the Rapture of the Church is to take place at the epiphany, not seven years earlier?

Certainly if one can make anything of language at all, no distinction can be made between the parousia, the apokalypse, and the epiphany of our Lord. They are one and the same event. Furthermore, as we have already indicated, although it is argued that the parousia means "presence" and therefore covers the entire period of time introduced by His coming to rapture the Church, it is clear from Scripture's use of the words apokalypse and epiphany that the Revelation of Christ is not an event which has to do exclusively with judgment. *It is also the day upon which the believer's hope is set when he will enter into the completed blessings of salvation at Christ's second coming.*

We can only conclude that the distinction between the Rapture of the Church and the Revelation of Christ is an inference which is nowhere asserted by the Word of God and not required by the teminology relating to the return of Christ. On the contrary, if any inference is to be drawn, the terminology suggests that the Revelation of Christ is, like the Rapture, the day of the believer's salvation when he enters into consummated fellowship with the Lord and receives his reward from the hand of the Lord. The parousia, the apokalypse, and the epiphany appear to be a single event. Any division of Christ's coming into two parts is an unproven inference.

The fact that even pretribulationists feel some embarrassment in trying to separate the second coming of Christ into two events or even into two separate parts may be seen in the contention of one of the most recent writers of this school who maintains that the return of Christ for His Church is not the second coming of Christ. This view makes a distinction between the *return* of Christ and His *second coming.* This is an utterly unwarranted distinction. No support is sought for it in the words used to describe Christ's return. The words "return" and "second coming" are not properly speaking Biblical words in that the two words do not represent any equivalent Greek words. There is no difference in the concepts conveyed to the mind by return and coming. It is in other words an artificial and impossible distinction. Christ's parousia is His return; His return is His coming; His coming is His second advent.

The vocabulary used of our Lord's return lends no support for the idea of two comings of Christ or of two aspects of His coming. On the contrary, it substantiates the view that the return of Christ will be a single, indivisible glorious event.

4

THE TRIBULATION, THE RAPTURE, AND THE RESURRECTION

WE TURN now to a consideration of the passages of Scripture which deal with the Great Tribulation, the Rapture of the Church, and the Resurrection to determine whether or not the Rapture and the Resurrection occur at the beginning or the end of the Tribulation.

Everyone agrees that the Scriptures teach that Christ will appear in glory at the end of the Tribulation. The Word of God is indisputably clear on this point. "Immediately after the tribulation of those days," cosmic signs and convulsions will occur. "Then shall appear the sign of the Son of man in heaven, and then shall all the tribes of the earth mourn, and they shall see the Son of man coming on the clouds of heaven with power and great glory" (Matt. 24:29, 31). The preceding chapter has discussed many verses which place the coming of Christ at the end of the Tribulation.

Furthermore, we have found no support in our study of the vocabulary used of Christ's return for the theory that before this glorious manifestation of Christ, He will come secretly to rapture the Church. Thus far, all evidence points to a single, indivisible coming of the Lord.

The natural assumption is that the Rapture of the Church and the Resurrection of the dead in Christ will take place at His glorious coming. The burden of proof rests on those who teach that this is not the proper order of events. We *know* Christ is coming at the end of the Tribulation. We *know* the living saints are to be caught up to be with Christ when He comes. We *know* the dead in Christ will be raised at His coming. The Word of God is clear on these points.

If we are to have equal certainty that the Rapture and the Resurrection do not occur at the coming of Christ at the end of the Tribulation but at a secret coming before the Tribulation begins, the Word of God should be equally clear. We cannot lend the authority of the Word of God to an assumption in light of which the Scripture is interpreted, unless such an assumption is explicitly taught or is demanded by the data of Scripture. If the Rapture is to precede the Tribulation, certainly some of the Scriptures which predict the Rapture and the Tribulation and the Resurrection should make clear this order of events. We must examine carefully these passages to determine what they teach.

In this chapter we shall first look at the three great passages which describe the Great Tribulation to discover if they place the coming of Christ and the Rapture of the Church at its beginning. Then we shall examine the passages which prophesy the Rapture to ask if this event is placed before the Tribulation. We shall turn then to the verses which deal with the resurrection of believers to see where this resurrection is located. Finally, we shall consider several single verses which are held to affirm the removal of the Church before the Tribulation.

We may be permitted to limit this study to the New Testament teaching, for pretribulationists assert that the Church does not appear in the Old Testament predictions. Since our study has to do with the Church and the Tribulation, any evidence deduced from the Old Testament would be considered irrelevant by pretribulationists.

The Great Tribulation in the Olivet Discourse

In the Olivet Discourse, our Lord sketched the course of this age (Matt. 24:4-14),[1] the events of the Great Tribulation including the coming of Antichrist who is called the

---

1. It is not important for our present discussion whether these verses sketch the course of the age as we believe, or refer to the first half of the period of Tribulation as some believe.

Abomination of Desolation (vv. 15-25), and the glorious second coming of the Son of Man (vv. 26-31). The only verse in this discourse which can possibly be construed to refer to the Rapture is verse 31, "And he shall send forth his angels with a great sound of a trumpet, and they shall gather together his elect from the four winds, from one end of heaven to the other."

There are elements of striking similarity between this verse and Paul's teaching about the Rapture of the Church. "For the Lord himself shall descend from heaven, with a shout, with the voice of the archangel, and with the trump of God (I Thess. 4:16). In both passages are mentioned the coming of Christ, the sounding of a trumpet, and the accompanying presence of angels. Furthermore, the word "gather together" (*episunago*) in Matthew 24:31 is the verb whose noun (*episunagoge*) is used in I Thessalonians 2:1 of our "gathering together" unto the Lord at the Rapture. If this is not the Rapture of the Church, then our Lord was altogether silent about this subject in His Olivet Discourse; and pretribulationists assert that this is indeed the case. It is, however, customary for many pretribulation teachers to *assume* that the Rapture is to be placed somewhere before verse 14 of Matthew 24, for "this gospel of the kingdom" is taken to be the announcement of the millennial, Davidic kingdom which is about to be established by the return of Christ, and whose establishment is to be proclaimed throughout all the world by a Jewish remnant after the Church has been raptured. There is, however, *no hint in the Gospels that this is the case.* The Rapture of the Church before the Tribulation is an *assumption;* it is not taught in the Olivet Discourse.

II Thessalonians 2

The coming of Antichrist and the persecution which he will inflict upon God's people are prophesied by Paul in II Thessalonians 2. Nowhere does Paul say that the Rapture of the Church is to precede these events. The prophecy of the Rapture of the Church in I Thessalonians 4 says nothing about the Tribulation. Indeed, as one reads the opening verses of the prophecy of Antichrist, one gains the impression that such events as the great apostasy and the appearance of the Man of Lawlessness are to take place before "the coming of our Lord Jesus Christ, and our gathering together unto him" (II Thess. 2:1). For if the Church is not to be in the world when the Man of Lawlessness appears, Paul's argument to the Thessalonians seems to be rather badly directed. In his first letter, Paul had taught them of the resurrection of the dead and the Rapture of the Church at the second coming of Christ. He did not assert that these events would precede the Tribulation. This letter created the reaction that the Day of the Lord had already come and that the end of the world was immediately at hand (II Thess. 2:2). If this "day of the Lord" is to be identified with the glorious Revelation of Christ at the end of the Tribulation, then Paul's argument in this prophecy has omitted its most important point, namely, that the Rapture is the first event which will take place; and since the Rapture had not taken place and the Thessalonian Christians were still on earth, it was impossible that the Day of the Lord had come. Such things as the apostasy and the appearance of the Man of Lawlessness could have only an academic interest for the Thessalonians if they were to be caught up from the earth before these events took place.

On the contrary, Paul writes as though Christians needed to be warned against the deception of the Antichrist, and he rejoices that God has chosen them from the beginning to be saved (vs. 13), not to perish through delusion by the Antichrist (vs. 10f). One would naturally conclude from reading Paul's words that the coming of the Lord, our gathering together unto Him, and the day of the Lord are one and the same event which will be preceded by the apostasy and the Man of Lawlessness. Since the Man of Lawlessness was not on the horizon, one might know that the day of the Lord had not yet come.

Paul's failure at this point to assert that the Rapture of the Church would be the first in this succession of events would be a surrender of his strongest argument to settle the Thessalonian problem. The day of the Lord could not possibly have come, for the Rapture had not taken place. Why did he not simply assert this to be true? He does not do so; there is no affirmation of a pretribulation rapture here.

The force of this line of reasoning may be illustrated by the attempt of a recent important study on pretribulationism to find the Rapture in this chapter in the word *apostasia*. The word is construed to mean "departure," i.e., the departure of the Church from earth in the Rapture. This rendition results in the following order of events: the departure (Rapture), Man of Lawlessness, the Revelation of Christ.

"Departure" is an unnatural rendition of *apostasia*. Before the book was published, this interpretation appeared in *Our Hope* and the reactions of a number of outstanding Christian teachers were solicited. Suffice it to say that a strong majority of the men consulted felt that this interpretation was extremely improbable. (See *Our Hope*, June, 1950).

Revelation 8-16

The third passage dealing with the Great Tribulation is in the book of Revelation, chapters 8 through 16, where we have the appearance of the Beast whom we call the Antichrist, the terrible persecution which he inflicts upon the saints of God, the sounding of the seven trumpets and the outpouring of the seven vials which constitute the Great Tribulation from the point of view of the divine judgment on the world. There is no pretribulation rapture in this prophecy. The only description of the second coming of Christ in the book of Revelation is His glorious coming in chapter 19; and the Rapture of the Church is altogether omitted. His coming is also mentioned in 1:7, 2:25.

Some students find the "door opened in heaven" and the
voice which said to John, "Come up hither" (Rev. 4:1) to
be a reference to the Rapture of the Church; but this is
interpretation, human opinion, and not the declaration of
Scripture. One of the most influential writers of this school
tells us that the Church is raptured between the close of
chapter 3 and the opening of chapter 4, but the Seer does
not record this event; he takes it for granted. This is just
the point. To find a pretribulation rapture in the book
which says most about the Great Tribulation, one must
take it for granted. The Word of God nowhere says that
the Rapture will precede the Tribulation.

The "rapture" of John in Revelation 4:1, if we may call
it that, is his way of indicating that he entered into an ec-
static experience when, "in the Spirit," he was given visions
of the last things. Paul speaks of a similar experience
when he was "caught up into the third heaven" (II Cor.
12:2). So completely overwhelmed was he, so utterly were
his faculties under the control of the Holy Spirit that he
was not sure whether he was "in the body or apart from
the body" (vs. 3). The open door and the voice from
heaven in Revelation 4:1 have nothing to do with the
Church but only with the experience of the Apostle.

The argument that the Church must be in heaven after
4:1 because the view-point of the book thereafter is heavenly does not reckon with the fact that John's heavenly
view-point is not sustained throughout the book. In 10:1,
John sees an angel "coming down out of heaven"; John is
now apparently on earth (see also 18:1). In chapter 11, he
is on earth to measure the Temple. But in 11:14ff., he is
in heaven again. In 13:1, he is on earth and sees the Beast
arising out of the sea; and in 14:1, he sees the 144,000 in
Jerusalem in the millennial kingdom. John's view-point
alternates between heaven and earth; but throughout the
entire experience, he is in ecstasy beholding visions im-
parted to him by the Spirit of God. Both view-points re-

fer to the subjective visions of the inspired Apostle and provide no clue for the interpretation of the book.

Our survey of these three great passages which set forth the coming of Antichrist and the Great Tribulation shows clearly that none of them asserts that the Church is to be raptured at the beginning of the Tribulation. When such a doctrine is attributed to these Scriptures, it is an inference and not the assertion of the Word of God.

The Rapture and the Tribulation

If a pretribulation rapture is a Biblical doctrine, it ought to be clearly set forth in the Scriptures which prophesy the Rapture of the Church. In fact, pretribulationists tell us that the Rapture is a mystery, first revealed to Paul; and we are led to assume that this mystery, this new truth now divinely disclosed is the *time* of the Rapture, viz., that it will occur before the Tribulation.

Only one passage in the Word of God describes the Rapture by name. Other passages describe the change which will take place in the living saints at that day, especially I Corinthians 15:51-53 and Philippians 3:20-21. The latter verse contains no indication of time and therefore contributes nothing to our study.

The Thessalonians were concerned about the fate of believers who died before the coming of Christ. Paul assures them that they need not sorrow as do men who have no hope. "For if we believe that Jesus died and rose again, even so them also that are fallen asleep in Jesus will God bring with him. For this we say to you by the word of the Lord, that we that are alive, that are left unto the coming of the Lord, shall in no wise precede them that are fallen asleep. For the Lord himself shall descend from heaven, with a shout, with the voice of the archangel, and with the trump of God: and the dead in Christ shall rise first; then we that are alive, that are left, shall together with them be caught up in the clouds, to meet the Lord in the air: and so shall we ever be with the Lord" (I Thess. 4:14-17).

The word "Rapture" is derived from the Latin word *rapio* which is found in the Latin Bible in verse 17 and translated "caught up." This Rapture will occur at the parousia of Jesus. The only aspect of the parousia which Paul has in mind is its relationship to believers. In this passage he says nothing about its relationship to the world. The parousia of Jesus in this passage has for its object union with all believers, whether they are dead or living. The dead "in Christ," i.e., believers only, will be raised in their glorious resurrection bodies. Then the remaining believers, those who are still alive, will be caught up, raptured, to meet the Lord in the air.

The Rapture means two things: 1). Union with the Lord. This is the thought emphasized in the Thessalonian epistle. Paul says nothing about the character of the resurrection body; in fact, he does not even mention it. He speaks only of blessed union with Christ. The emphasis in this meeting is not upon the place — in the air. Pretribulationists place the emphasis here and insist that Jesus does not come to the earth. This, however, is not asserted by the Scripture. *Nothing is said about what happens immediately after the meeting.* It is just as possible, and, as we shall show later on, even suggested by the word used for the "meeting," that after this meeting, Jesus continues His descent to the earth, but now accompanied by His saints. The one point of emphasis is the fact of union — we are raptured to meet the Lord. Thus shall we ever be *with the Lord*, whether in the air, in heaven, or on earth.

This meeting is illustrated in the parable of the virgins. They were waiting for the hour of the wedding feast. When the bridegroom approached, they went out to meet him and then accompanied him into the marriage feast. The Rapture has as its first objective the union of the living Church with her returning Lord.

2). The second significance of the Rapture is the transformation of the bodies of living believers. The Rapture is not only the moment of union with Christ when faith is translated into sight; it is the symbol of the redemption of the body (Rom. 8:23). The resurrection of the dead saints is not a revivification, i.e., a return to the level of experience and to the conditions which prevailed during mortal life on earth. Lazarus apparently experienced such a resurrection. He was restored to physical life and, we may assume, died again after filling out the natural span of life. His was a *physical* resurrection.

The resurrection of saints at the parousia of Christ is not a physical resurrection, although it is a bodily resurrection. It is not a restoration to physical life; it is an introduction into a new level of life which transforms the very bodily existence. At His coming, Christ will "fashion anew (literally, metamorphose) the body of our humiliation that it may be conformed to the body of his glory" (Phil. 3:21). Our Lord's resurrection body was the same and yet very different from His physical body. It was a real body, visible, palpable, recognizable; and yet it moved on a higher level of life. Apparently, from our Gospel accounts, we are to conclude that it no longer was limited to what we call natural laws. Jesus could go and come at will as He never did in the days of His flesh.

So will it be with the resurrection body of believers. Paul describes it as an incorruptible, glorious, powerful, spiritual body (I Cor. 15:42-44). This is not a body made out of spirit or constituted of spirit; it is a body completely infused by the power and quickened by the life of the Holy Spirit, a body perfectly designed for the enjoyment of eternal life. What a glorious realization that even our bodies are to be redeemed from weakness, pain, decay and death.

This transformation will occur for the dead saints at the first resurrection; it will occur for the living saints at the Rapture. The Rapture, the catching up to meet the Lord in the air, is the sign that the living, as well as the dead, have put on the glorious resurrection body. They are no longer earthbound, mortal creatures but have entered into the fullness of life, which means a new level of existence whose character we can now only faintly discern. "We shall not all sleep (in death), but we shall all (dead and living saints) be changed . . . the dead shall be raised incorruptible, and we (the living) shall be changed" (I Cor. 15:51-52).

This glorious event, the Rapture of the Church, is a mystery (I Cor. 15:51). A mystery is a divine truth, purposed by God ages ago, but revealed to men only in due time (Rom. 16:25-26). *The mystery of the Rapture is not the time of the Rapture* as pretribulationists assume; it is the *fact of the Rapture*. God had never before revealed to men what would be the particular lot of the living saints at the end of the age. The doctrine of resurrection had long been taught (cf. Dan. 12:2), but the fact that the living are to put on their resurrection bodies at the moment of Christ's return without passing through death and join the resurrected dead in the presence of Christ is revealed for the first time through the Apostle Paul. There is an intimation of it, we believe, in Matthew 24:31 when Jesus spoke of the angels gathering the elect from the four corners of the earth; but this prophecy lacks the details which give to the Rapture its specific character. *How* the elect are to be gathered together is not indicated by our Lord.

The mystery of the Rapture therefore is not the truth that the Rapture is to occur before the Great Tribulation. It is the *fact* that the living dead will be bodily transformed at Jesus' parousia and as a result of the transformation will be caught up to meet the Lord in the air and so be ever with the Lord. There is no affirmation in the Scripture that the Rapture will take place before the Tribulation begins. Such a teaching is an inference, not the assertion of the Word of God.

The Resurrection and the Tribulation

If the teaching of a pretribulation rapture is in the Word of God, it ought to be asserted in the passages where the doctrine of the resurrection is set forth; for according to pretribulationism, the resurrection of the righteous will occur before the Great Tribulation takes place. Pretribulationism in effect divides the resurrection into three parts: the first resurrection (Rev. 20:4-5) — the resurrection of all the saints, which will occur at the coming of Christ *for* His Church at the beginning of the Great Tribulation; the resurrection of the tribulation martyrs at the end of the Tribulation; and the second resurrection at the end of the millennium (Rev. 20:12-15). The martyr-resurrection is, according to pretribulationism, a part of the first resurrection.

If in fact the first resurrection is divided into two parts, the first part, the resurrection of the saints, occurring at the time of the Rapture of the Church before the Tribulation, and the second part, the resurrection of martyrs at the end of the Tribulation, the Word of God ought to make this clear. *The two stages of the first resurrection should be as clear as the fact of the two resurrections.*

Amillennialists deny that there are in fact two resurrections. They speak of the General Resurrection of all the dead. However, the teaching of two resurrections is a clear assertion of Scripture, and the teaching of a single resurrection must pass over several important passages in the Word. The Revelation speaks explicitly of a first resurrection at the beginning of the millennium, and it then describes a second resurrection at the end of the millennium (Rev. 20:4-15). Any interpretation of this first resurrection which spiritualizes it and refuses to see a bodily resurrection of the same sort as the second resurrection does not do justice to the demands of language.[2] Two literal bodily resurrections are demanded.

---

2. Cf. the author's book, *Crucial Questions Concerning the Kingdom of God* (Grand Rapids: Eerdmans, 1952), Chapter 7.

This twofold character of the resurrection is also suggested elsewhere in the Scriptures. Our Lord spoke of a resurrection of life (the first resurrection), and a resurrection of judgment (the second resurrection, Jn. 5:29). He spoke of the resurrection of the just as though it was to be distinguished from the resurrection of the unjust (Lk. 14:14). He spoke of those "that are accounted worthy to attain to that age, and the resurrection from the dead" (literally, the resurrection which is from dead ones, Lk. 20:35), indicating that it is a resurrection of some of the dead which will be an attainment of a favored group who have been accounted worthy of this particular blessing. Similarly, Paul's hope for the future is set not upon a general resurrection — a doctrine which he would have held as a Pharisee (Acts 23:6), but upon the attainment to the "out-resurrection which is from dead ones" (Phil. 3:11). At the parousia, not the dead in general, but "they that are Christ's" will be raised (I Cor. 15:23). All of these passages reinforce the teaching of Revelation 20 that there will be two resurrections of the dead. This is not an inference but the explicit affirmation of Scripture, reinforced by other Scriptures which have inferential value.

Does the Word similarly teach that the first resurrection will consist of two stages, the first of which will occur at the beginning of the Tribulation? No such teaching appears in the Scripture. Notes of time which define the resurrection are very few. The resurrection will occur at "the last day" (Jn. 6:39, 40, 44, 54; 11:24). A reference to the resurrection is included in Paul's longing for the transformation of the body at the coming of Christ (Phil. 3:20-21), but the time is not clearly stated. References to the resurrection are found in Romans 6:5, 8:11, II Timothy 2:18, Acts 17:18, 24:15, Hebrews 6:2, 11:35, but no indications of time enable us to place the resurrection before the Tribulation.

Other references having more specific temporal reference are I Corinthians 15:23, where it occurs at the parousia of our Lord, and I Thessalonians 4:16, where it occurs when the Lord descends from heaven; but these passages say nothing about the relationship of the resurrection to the Tribulation. The question of the time of the parousia will be discussed below.

The one passage which explicitly locates the first resurrection is the prophecy in Revelation 20, and this is also *the only passage which describes the resurrection of martyrs.* In chapter 19, Christ comes on a white horse as a victorious conqueror to destroy the Antichrist and to punish the kings who supported him. After the battle of Armageddon occurs the resurrection. John saw two groups of people: he saw thrones and people seated upon them to whom judgment was given. John says little about this first group because his main concern is with those who have been slain by Antichrist. He at once singles out for special attention this second group: the souls of them who had been martyred by the Beast in the Great Tribulation. *Both groups come to life at the same time* in the first resurrection.

The identity of the second group is clear. But who are contained in the first, undefined group? Only one possibility commends itself. They are the righteous who have died naturally, who have not been martyred. They are the saints in general, the "dead in Christ" (I Thess. 4:16). To say that this resurrection occurred back before chapter 4 is contradicted by the clear assertion of the passage: "They came to life" (vs. 4). The subject of the verb is both groups — those seated on thrones, and the martyrs. There is no mention or suggestion of a resurrection earlier than the glorious return of Christ at the end of the Tribulation, and this passage locates the resurrection both of saints and martyrs at the *Revelation* of Christ.

The teaching that a resurrection of saints takes place at the beginning of the Tribulation is an assumption utterly unsupported by the Scriptures that teach resurrection, and it is contradicted by Revelation 20.

1 Thessalonians 5:9

We must consider finally a number of verses which are held by pretribulationists to teach that the Church will be removed from the world before the Tribulation occurs. In I Thessalonians 5:9, Paul says, "For God appointed us not unto wrath, but unto the obtaining of salvation through our Lord Jesus Christ." Since the Great Tribulation is to consist in part of the outpouring of God's wrath upon a decadent and sinful society (Rev. 16:1), and since God has not appointed His people to experience wrath, must we not conclude that the Church is to be removed before God's wrath is poured out upon the earth?

We hasten here to agree that the Church which Christ has redeemed by His precious blood will never experience the wrath of God. If the question of the Rapture and the Tribulation is to be settled on this issue alone, the only alternative is a pretribulation rapture, for the Church will never suffer God's wrath.

However, this admission does not lead to pretribulationism, for the verse in question says nothing about either the Rapture or the Tribulation. All it asserts is that the Church will not fall under God's wrath. The wrath in question may not refer to the Tribulation at all, but to God's wrath in the final judgment (Rom. 2:5). However, if it does include the Great Tribulation, the verse neither asserts nor suggests that the Church will be *removed* from the world; it is only promised deliverance.

The Israelites were in Egypt during the visitation of the plagues upon the Egyptians but they were sheltered from the worst of these plagues which befell the Egyptians. In a similar way it is possible that the Church may find herself on earth during the period of the Tribulation but will by divine protection be sheltered from the sufferings entailed by the outpouring of the bowls of wrath and thus be delivered from the wrath to come. *I Thessalonians* 5:9 *says nothing about the Rapture.* That it does is an unjustified inference. It says only that the Church will be delivered from wrath. How the deliverance is to be effected is not suggested. If the Church is on earth during the Great Tribulation but is divinely sheltered from wrath, this verse is fulfilled. This is all it asserts.

Revelation 3:10

This verse appears at first sight to teach a pretribulation rapture. "Because thou didst keep the word of my patience, I also will keep thee from the hour of trial, that hour which is to come upon the whole world, to try them that dwell upon the earth." This prophecy refers to the Great Tribulation, and it is directed not against God's people but against the "earth-dwellers." This phrase is a recurring one in the Revelation by which the author designates the people of a godless society who have surrendered themselves to the worship of Antichrist and who are to suffer the wrath of God (cf. 6:10, 8:13, 11:10, 13:8, 14, 17:8). The language of this verse, taken by itself, could be interpreted to teach complete escape from the coming hour of Tribulation. The language is, "I will keep thee *out of* the hour of trial" (*tereso ek*).

This language, however, neither asserts nor demands the idea of bodily removal from the midst of the coming trial. This is proven by the fact that precisely the same words are used by our Lord in His prayer that God would keep His disciples "out of the evil" (*Tereses ek tou ponerou*, Jn. 17:15). In our Lord's prayer, there is no idea of bodily removal of the disciples from the evil world but of preservation from the power of evil even when they are in its very presence. A similar thought occurs in Galatians 1:4, where we read that Christ gave Himself for our sins to deliver us from (literally, "out of," *ek*) this present evil age. This does not refer to a physical removal from the age but to deliverance from its power and control. "This age" will not pass away until the return of Christ.

In the same way, the promise of Revelation 3:10 of being kept *ek* the hour of trial need not be a promise of a removal from the very physical presence of tribulation. It is a promise of preservation and deliverance in and through it. This verse neither asserts that the Rapture is to occur before the Tribulation, nor does its interpretation require us to think that such a removal is intended.

Luke 21:36

A third verse which appears to teach bodily deliverance from the Tribulation and thus to suggest a pretribulation rapture is Luke 21:36. "But watch ye at every season, making supplication, that ye may prevail to escape all these things that shall come to pass, and to stand before the Son of Man." Many teachers assume that "all these things" refers to everything which will occur during the period of the Great Tribulation. However, we must ask, Is this a mere assumption, or does the Word actually teach it? Does "all of these things" refer to the persecutions of the Great Tribulation which shall be inflicted upon the people of God by the Abomination of Desolation — a persecution which is described in Matthew 24:15 through 22?

This eschatological persecution by the Antichrist of the "elect" recorded in Matthew is not recorded by Luke. Instead, Luke relates the words of our Lord pertaining to the destruction of Jerusalem which occurred in 70 A. D. In the verses which follow (25-28), Jesus announced the events which would immediately precede His second coming. There will be signs in the heavens and distress among the nations as men are filled with foreboding over "the things which are coming on the world" (v. 26). The context makes it clear that this fear is caused by the expectation of divine judgment, of God's wrath, "for the powers of the heaven will be shaken." The thought is not greatly expanded; but it clearly has to do with supernatural events which will attend the return of the Son of Man with power and great glory. Then we meet the striking statement, "Now when these things begin to take place, look up and lift your heads, because your redemption draweth nigh"

(v. 28). The events which indicate the imminent coming of Christ strike fear to the hearts of some but hope to the hearts of others, who see in these very signs the promise of coming redemption. This verse excludes the idea of a secret, any-moment coming of Christ. Recognizable signs are to precede His return to herald its near approach.

Then, as in Matthew, we read a warning against lapsing into spiritual stupor, "lest that day come on you suddenly like a snare" (v. 34). From the context, "that day" can be nothing but the day of the glorious coming of Christ which will bring judgment to all mankind (v. 35). In light of this impending judgment, spiritual alertness is imperative. Therefore Jesus warned, "But watch ye at every season, making supplication, that ye may prevail to escape all these things that shall come to pass, and to stand before the Son of man." The antecedent of "all these things" which the watchful will escape is found in verse 26, "the things which are coming on the world" which strike fear to the hearts of man — the divine judgments which will be inflicted at the return of Christ. The world is to fear the judgments of God's wrath which will accompany "that day," but the watching believer need not fear them. It is indeed these judgments which those who are spiritually awake will escape.

This promise has nothing to do with the Tribulation described in Matthew 24:21 which involves persecution of God's elect by Antichrist. The parallel verse to Luke 21:26 is not Matthew 24:21f., which describes the persecution of Antichrist during the Great Tribulation, but Matthew 24:29, 30, which describes the judgment which will fall at the end of the Tribulation at the appearing of the Son of man. Then, all the tribes of the earth will mourn because of the impending judgment. "Immediately after the tribulation of those days shall the sun be darkened, and the moon shall not give her light, and the stars shall fall from heaven, and the powers of the heavens shall be shaken. And then shall appear the sign of the Son of man in heaven;

and then shall the tribes of the earth mourn, and they shall see the Son of man coming in the clouds of heaven with power and great glory . . . . But know this, that if the master of the house had known in what watch the thief would come, he would have watched, and would not have suffered his house to be broken through" (Matt. 24:29, 30, 43). Those who are spiritually asleep will suffer judgment; but those who are "watching," that is, who are spiritually awake, will escape judgment and will stand before the Son of Man.

Luke 21:36 has nothing to do with the question of the Rapture of the Church. It is a promise that God's people will not be subjected to the divine judgments which will fall upon an evil world at the second advent of Christ. We have already met this promise in Revelation 3:10 and I Thessalonians 5:9. It was also given by our Lord.

We have now completed our survey of the passages which have to do with the Tribulation, the Rapture, and the Resurrection. Nowhere is the Rapture placed before the Tribulation. On the contrary, problems of exegesis are frequently raised if it is assumed that the Rapture precedes the Tribulation. Most of the Scriptures contain no specific temporal references as to the relation of these events. We must again emphatically point out that nowhere does the Word of God affirm that the Rapture and the Resurrection of believers will precede the Tribulation. The one passage which contains clear indications of time is Revelation 20, and it places the resurrection at the end of the Tribulation at the coming of Christ in glory. Pretribulationism is an inference in light of which Scripture is interpreted. It is not supported by any affirmations in the Word of God.

5

A VALID INFERENCE?

WE HAVE now examined the terminology used of our
Lord's coming and have found no support for the
idea that the return of Christ will be divided into two aspects — one before and one after the Tribulation. We have
studied the passages which deal with the Tribulation, the
Rapture and the Resurrection and have found that nowhere in these passages does the Word of God place the
Rapture before the Tribulation. On the contrary, the Resurrection is placed after the Tribulation in the Revelation.

Pretribulationism is in fact an inference in light of which
the Scriptural teachings about the second coming of
Christ and the attending events are interpreted. We must
now examine the most important bases of this inference to
determine if it is a necessary and valid one. We will admit that even if Scripture did not explicitly affirm a pretribulation rapture, it is possible that the totality of Scriptural data would demand such a conclusion; and in this
case, it would be a valid inference. There are in fact many
positions accepted in theology which are inferential in character. The bases for such inferences must be closely examined. If it turns out that the reasons for the inference
of pretribulationism are equally susceptible to another interpretation, we shall be compelled to conclude that it is an
unnecessary or even an invalid inference, especially since
the Scriptural data already covered point towards a posttribulation rapture.

Coming For and With the Saints

The phrases most commonly used to sustain pretribulationism are those which describe Christ's coming "for His

saints" and "with His saints." At the Rapture, Christ comes for the saints that He may catch up the living and raise the dead saints to meet Him in the air. In I Thessalonians 3:13, Paul spoke of the parousia of the Lord Jesus with all His saints. It is argued that it is impossible for Christ to come *with* His saints unless He has first come *for* them. There must have been a previous gathering of the saints unto Christ in the air that He now comes to earth accompanied by the saints. Therefore, the Rapture must occur in advance of Christ's coming with the saints and be a separate event.

This interpretation possesses a deceptive simplicity. On the face of it, it appears very persuasive, but it by no means proves a pretribulation rapture. What does the Word mean when it says that Christ will come "with His saints?" The word "saints" means "holy ones," and may not refer to men at all but to the event described by our Lord in Mark 8:38, "For whosoever shall be ashamed of me and my words in this adulterous and sinful generation, the Son of Man shall also be ashamed of him when he cometh in the glory of his father with the *holy* angels." The phrase in I Thessalonians 3, literally translated reads, "with all his holy ones," and may mean His holy angels. This at least was the opinion of one of the editors of the Scofield Reference Bible, William J. Erdman. Of this verse, Erdman said, "These saints or holy ones are the angels who in other scriptures are said to come with the Lord; they accompany him when he comes for the church as in this verse." If the "holy ones" of this verse are angels, then it cannot be used to support a pretribulation rapture.

But even if the phrase does refer to redeemed men, which we feel is more likely, it still provides no necessary support for the idea of two aspects of Christ's coming. The most natural meaning of the passage is that it refers to the same event described in I Thessalonians 4:14: "For if we believe that Christ died and rose again, even so them also that are fallen asleep in Jesus will God bring *with him*."

This "coming with Christ" is simultaneous with the Rapture and the Resurrection as this verse indicates and is not an event which will occur at a considerable time after the Rapture. When Christ returns at the time of the Rapture, those who are dead in Christ God will bring with Him.

Paul's thought may be understood by turning to the word used of *meeting* the Lord in the air, *apantesis*. This noun is used in only three other places in the New Testament. We find it used of the second coming of Christ in the parable of the virgins who were waiting for the hour of the wedding when the bridegroom would come. Finally the cry is raised, "Behold, the bridegroom! come ye forth to *meet* him" (Matt. 25:6). The virgins then went out to meet the approaching bridegroom and immediately returned, accompanying him to the wedding. The word is again used of Paul's visit to Rome. As he approached the city, some of the brethren heard of his approach and they went out to *meet* him outside of the city and so accompanied him as he entered Rome (Acts 28:15,16).

In the same way, the second coming of Christ will be a coming which is at the same time a coming *for* His saints and a coming *with* them. The Rapture of the Church is essentially an indication of the transformation of living believers into their glorious resurrection bodies without passing through death. They are caught up from the earth to be with the Lord and thus enter into the new realm of their glorified existence along with the resurrected dead. Thereafter they shall ever be with the Lord, and they accompany Him as He continues on to the earth. There is no ground whatsoever to assume that there must be a considerable interval of time between the Rapture and Christ's coming with His Church. They may be two aspects of a single indivisible event. In any case the phraseology of Christ's coming for His saints and with His saints is no proof for the inference that these are two separate events divided by a number of years. Such an inference may be drawn, but it is a human interpretation, not the clear assertion of the

Word of God. Other interpretations are equally possible. There is no proof here of a pretribulation rapture.

Day of Christ, Day of the Lord

Appeal for support of this inference is also made to the phrases "the day of Christ" and "the day of the Lord." It is maintained that these are two different days. The day of Christ refers to the time of Christ's coming to rapture the Church before the Tribulation when He will bestow rewards upon His people. The day of the Lord is always a day of judgment and has reference to the apokalypse of Christ at the end of the Tribulation to bring the visitation of judgment upon the world. Thus when we read of the events attending the day of the Lord in II Thessalonians 2:2, we are not to think of the Rapture of the Church, for the day of the Lord refers to the apokalypse of Christ for judgment at the end of the Tribulation. The Church has already been raptured.

The day of Christ is indeed a day of blessing and reward, and the day to which the believer eagerly looks forward (Phil. 1:6, 1:10, 2:16). It is also true that the day of the Lord will be a fearful day of judgment (Acts 2:20, II Thess. 2:2,8). This acknowledgment, however, by no means supports the inference that these are two different days separated by the period of the Tribulation.

In II Thessalonians, the day of the Lord is the day of the parousia of our Lord Jesus Christ and our gathering together unto him (II Thess. 2:1-2). In I Thessalonians, after describing the parousia of Christ to rapture the Church and raise the dead, Paul adds that there is no need for instruction as to the times and seasons, "for yourselves know perfectly that the day of the Lord so cometh as a thief in the night" (I Thess. 5:2). The world will be saying "peace and safety" but there shall come upon them sudden destruction. Believers, however, "are not in darkness, that that day should overtake you as a thief" (v. 4). The day of the Lord will not come upon believers unawares; "so then let us . . . watch and be sober" (v. 6). Believers are to "watch" with reference to the day of the Lord. It will be a day of surprise only for the world; Christians will be prepared for it, for they will not be asleep. The day of the Lord will for the Church mean salvation; for the world it will mean wrath (vv. 8 and 9). Certainly this language suggests that the day of the Lord whose coming Paul warns about in chapter five is the same as the parousia of Christ for the Rapture and the resurrection; otherwise the exhortation has no point. If the Rapture has already taken place before the day of the Lord, then Paul could not say, "But ye, brethren, are not in darkness, that that day should overtake you as a thief" (vs. 4), for "that day," the day of the Lord, will not overtake believers at all; they will be in heaven, raptured. According to pretribulationism, they do not need to "watch and be sober" for the day of the Lord but for the day of Christ; but this passage is concerned not with the day of Christ, but with the day of the Lord. Surely Paul's warning to believers to be prepared for the day of the Lord means that they will *see* that day but will not be surprised and dismayed by it. The warning is without point unless believers are to see that day; and if so, the day of Christ and the day of the Lord are synonymous.

The identity of the day of the Lord and of the day of Christ is further substantiated by the conflation of these two phrases. God will confirm His people unto the end that they may be unreprovable "in the *day* of our *Lord* Jesus Christ" (I Cor. 1:8). The day of Jesus Christ and the day of the Lord are one and the same day, the day of Christian expectation. Christians are to find delight in one another "in the day of our Lord Jesus" (II Cor. 1:14). Here again the object of Christian expectation is the day which is both the day of the Lord and the day of Jesus.

Where does the Word of God assert that the day of Christ is to be distinguished from the day of the Lord? Where does it say that the day of Christ occurs before the Tribulation

while the day of the Lord occurs at its end? These are inferences of good and godly men, but not the clear teaching
of the Word of God. If any inference is to be drawn, we
must infer that the two expressions refer to one and the
same day which will bring salvation to the Church but
judgment to the world.

Removal of the Holy Spirit

Another basis for the inference that the Church will be
raptured before the Tribulation is the claim that the Word
of God teaches that the Holy Spirit is to be taken out of the
world before the Tribulation begins; and since the Holy
Spirit indwells the Church, we must conclude that the
Church will be taken out of the world when the Holy Spirit
is removed.

This teaching is found in II Thessalonians 2:6, 7: "and
now ye know that which restraineth, to the end that he
may be revealed in his own season. For the mystery of
lawlessness doeth already work; only there is one that restraineth now until he be taken out of the way." Pretribulationism quite universally maintains that "the one that
restraineth now" is the Holy Spirit. The mystery of lawlessness is already working in the world, but the Spirit of
God who indwells the Church exercises a restraining power
upon lawlessness. There will come a day when this will no
longer be true and when the restraint is removed. This
can refer, we are told, only to a removal of the Holy Spirit
from the world in the Rapture of the Church.

This however is a human interpretation. The Word of
God does not say that the Holy Spirit is the restrainer. In
fact, this is a very difficult passage, for Paul is speaking
in very concise language which was intelligible to the Thessalonians because Paul had already taught them in person,
but it is very difficult for us. We must content ourselves
with pointing out that the passage says nothing at all about
the Holy Spirit. That it refers to the Holy Spirit is nothing

more than an inference. Nor does it say anything about the Rapture of the Church.

A different and a much more natural interpretation is the following. The expression "until he be taken out of the way" (literally "until he come out of the midst") may not refer to the restraining power at all but to the Antichrist. In this case the restraining power is the power of God Himself. The passage might be paraphrased, "for the mystery of lawlessness already is working; only there is the one who restrains now, namely God, until he, the Antichrist, arises out of the midst." This is precisely what verse six says. "And now do you know that which restraineth, to the end that he (the Antichrist) may be revealed in his own time." Verses six and seven thus say the same thing and there is a similar balance in the two parts of verses six and seven.

6a And now ye know that which restraineth
>(the power of God)

6b to the end that he may be revealed in his own season.
>(Antichrist)

For the mystery of lawlessness doth already work:

7a Only there is one that restraineth now
>(God)

7b until he come out of the midst.
>(Antichrist)

We readily admit that this is a human interpretation and is not authoritative. But it is at least as possible as the interpretation that the restraining one is the Holy Spirit, and it fits the movement of the passage more naturally. In any case, any support for a pretribulation rapture from this passage is nothing more than an assumption. The Scripture says nothing about a removal of the Holy Spirit or a Rapture of the Church. It is an inference and not an assertion of the Word of God.

The Teaching of the Revelation. Pretribulationists find ground for the inference of a pretribulation rapture in the book of Revelation. This ground is twofold. First, it is claimed that the Church is seen in heaven in the twenty-four elders (4:4) ; and second, the word "church" appears frequently in the first three chapters but not at all in chapters four to nineteen. We must therefore conclude that the Church is no longer on earth; it has been raptured and taken to heaven. The "saints" seen in the Tribulation are not the Church but either the Jewish remnant or men converted in the Tribulation by the world-wide proclamation of the "Gospel of the Kingdom" by this Jewish remnant.

The Twenty-four elders. Pretribulationalists claim that the twenty-four elders are the Church in heaven, for they are clothed in white, they are crowned, and they are seated upon thrones. If the Church is seen in heaven, we must conclude that it has already been raptured.

This however is an inference; we are not told that the twenty-four elders are the Church. The elders may represent the Church and yet involve no idea of a previous rapture. Many scholars see in the elders the *ideal* Church — an anticipation of the final state of things (Alford, Swete, Lange). The fact that the elders are clothed in white, crowned with *stephanoi* — the victor's wreath to be awarded to the Church at the *bema* of Christ — and seated on thrones does not prove that they are the Church after it has been raptured and rewarded. White is the array of angels (Matt. 28:3, John 20:12, Acts 1:10). The distinction between *stephanos*, the victor's wreath, and *diadema*, the ruler's crown, is not always followed. *Stephanos* is used of the ruler's crown in the Greek Bible at II Samuel 12:30, I Chronicles 20:2, Jeremiah 13:18, Esther 8:15 and elsewhere. The use of *stephanos* of the twenty-four elders does not prove that they are the Church which has received their rewards after the Rapture; the crowns may be symbolic of rule, not reward.

In the Old Testament, God is sometimes pictured surrounded by a council of heavenly beings (Ps. 89:6-8). Paul refers to angels as "thrones, principalities, rulers" (Col. 1:16, Romans 8:38, Eph. 3:10). So the twenty-four elders may be angelic beings who are pictured as executing the divine rule of the universe. This interpretation agrees with the fact that John addresses one of the elders as his superior (7:14), with the same deference which he displays toward angels (19:9, 22:8). And like the angel, the elder is sent to interpret one of John's visions (7:14). Probably therefore the elders are angels (Zahn); but if they do represent the Church, nothing is said whatsoever or intimated about a rapture.

Some have interpreted the open door and the voice calling, "Come up hither" to symbolize the Rapture (4:1); but the voice was addressed to John, not to the Church, and the open door is associated with the visions given to John. One of the most influential pretribulation commentators on Revelation says that the Rapture occurs *between* chapters three and four, but John passes over it in silence leaving his readers to assume that it has taken place. However, if we are to interpret Scripture by assumption, we can find almost anything we desire in the Word of God by assuming it is there.

Evidence for the identification of the elders with the Church is sought in the rendering of the King James Version of 5:9 where the elders sing a new song to the Lamb "who hast redeemed us to God by thy blood out of every kindred, tongue and people and nation; and hast made us unto our God kings and priests, and we shall reign on the earth." In this song, the elders appear to be the Church for they are identified as those redeemed by the blood of the Lamb, who are to share Christ's millennial reign.

This however is misleading, for the Authorized Version does not give us the correct form of the song. The American Revised Version, followed by the Williams and Verkuyl editions and most other modern translations, correctly renders their song, "for thou didst purchase unto God with thy blood *men* of every tribe, and tongue, and people, and nation and madest them *to be* unto our God a kingdom and priests and they reign upon the earth." The elders themselves are not the redeemed, but they sing of those who are redeemed. A distinction is thus made between the two groups. This use of the third person is not to be explained merely by the fact that the four living creatures join in the song, for in 11:18 the elders again distinguish themselves from the prophets and saints and all who fear God's name. Rather than supporting the identification, the evidence distinctly differentiates the elders from those who are redeemed through the blood of the Lamb. In 14:3, the elders are a third time set over against those who have been purchased out of the earth, who sing a new song which the elders cannot learn. Whoever they are, the Word of God does not say that they represent the raptured Church in heaven during the Tribulation. This is an unwarranted inference without support by the Scripture.

The Use of the Word "Church." The contention that the fact that the word "church" occurs many times in chapters one and three of Revelation and not at all in chapters four through twenty suggests that the book does not deal with the Church but with the Jewish period of the Tribulation after the Rapture of the Church is a tenuous inference, not a declaration of inspired Scripture.

"Church" occurs nineteen times in chapters one to three. It occurs four times in chapter one and in each instance it is a specific reference to "the seven churches" of Asia. It is used in the introduction of each of the seven letters in the address, "To the angel of the church in Ephesus," etc.; and it occurs at the conclusion of each of the letters in the phrase, "he that hath an ear, let him hear what the Spirit saith to the churches." The reference in 2:23 "to all the churches" refers to all of the seven churches in Asia Minor. The word "church" therefore is never used in the Revelation *to designate the Church in its totality;* it is employed only of the several historical churches to which John sent the seven letters and the Revelation itself.

One could reason with equal plausibility that the consummation in chapters nineteen and twenty has nothing to do with the Church, for the word "church" is nowhere found in the concluding chapters except in 22:16. To be sure, the bride of Christ is seen in 19:6-9; but it is *not called the Church*. If the argument is sound that the "saints" of 13:7, 10; 16:6; 17:6; 18:24 who suffer at the hands of Antichrist are not the Church because the word is not used and because we are on Jewish ground, then the bride of 19:6 cannot be the Church because the word is not used; the people involved are called *saints* (vs. 8). Furthermore, the bride is called the Lamb's wife. Pretribulationists usually distinguish between the concepts of wife and bride. "Israel is Jehovah's earthly wife; the Church is the Lamb's heavenly bride." But in Revelation 19:7, the bride is the Lamb's wife; and if we are indeed on Jewish ground, this term ought to refer only to Israel. However, pretribulationists agree that the bride is the Church. One very important fact they do not recognize: the marriage feast does not occur until after the return of Christ in glory.

The Marriage of the Lamb. Pretribulationists appeal to the picture of the marriage feast in Revelation 19:6-9 to prove a pretribulation rapture. We are told that in this vision, the Church is seen in the presence of Christ, arrayed for the marriage banquet, and this position of the Church at His return requires a Rapture at an earlier time — before the Great Tribulation, else the Church would not be in heaven prepared for the feast.

We must look at the passage closely, and when we do, we discover that Revelation 19:6-9 is a *prophetic* hymn of the marriage supper of the Lamb and not an actual portrayal of that event.

Practically all interpreters agree that this refers to the union of Christ and His Church. The picture of a wedding feast pictures the joy of this union. It is the day when believers are presented to Christ as a bride to her groom (Eph. 5:27). It represents the restoration of the fellowship Jesus enjoyed with His disciples in the days of His flesh (Mark 14:25). Our Lord used the picture of a wedding feast several times to describe the joy of the future kingdom (Matt. 22:1-14; 25:1-13; Luke 14:15-24). This is an event which pretribulationists hold will take place at the Rapture. "At the Rapture He appears as the Bridegroom to take His Bride to Himself. At the Revelation He will come with His Bride to establish His reign over all the earth." In the prophecy of Revelation 19, this glad day is at hand. The Church which has been betrothed to Christ and has lived in a hostile world in faithfulness and devotion to her Beloved now is about to realize the object of her hope — union with her Lord.

The time of the wedding feast is specifically indicated. *The wedding, the reunion with Christ, occurs at the Revelation of Christ in glory.* The feast does not actually occur in chapter 19. The prophetic hymn is not a description of the marriage; it is a *hymn of anticipation.* John beholds in vision what actually takes place in chapter 20.

This prophetic character of the hymn is proved by the first line: "Hallelujah; for the Lord our God, the Almighty, reigneth" (vs. 6). This reign has not yet begun; it is about to begin. Students of Greek speak of the form of this verb as an ingressive aorist, and the meaning is, "The Lord our God . . . has begun his reign." But the announcement is proleptic. The reign actually begins only after Christ appears as the victorious conqueror on the white horse, clad in a warrior's battle-stained garments for the battle of Armageddon (16:16; 19:17-18). Only after the destruction of the Beast and the False Prophet, together with the kings who served them (19:19-21), and the binding and imprisonment of the Devil does the kingdom come and the reign announced in 19:6 actually begin.

The prophetic hymn sings of this reign as though it had already taken place, for it is actually about to occur. This proclamation of impending events occurs frequently in the Revelation. A prophetic announcement of the kingdom is found in 11:15, "The kingdom of the world is become the kingdom of our Lord and of his Christ; and he shall reign for ever and ever." This proclamation of the coming millennial kingdom occurs before the out-pouring of the seven bowls, before the sounding of the seven trumpets, before the appearance of Antichrist. Yet the announcement is heralded in the past tense as though it were an already accomplished fact. Chapter 14 is a series of such proleptic announcements. The 144,000 are seen standing on Mt. Zion in the millennial kingdom. The fall of Babylon, the capital city of Antichrist, is announced as though it had already occurred. The harvest of both the righteous and the unrighteous is proclaimed. All of these events are to take place in the future; but the end is so near and the events so certain that they were announced as though they were already history.

Such is the character of the prophetic hymn of chapter 19. We stand at the very threshold of the event. Babylon has been destroyed (18); civil strife has arisen within the kingdom of Antichrist (17:16-18) and economic chaos results. Now the King is about to appear and give the final death blow to Antichrist; and then He will begin His glorious reign, the reign of the millennial kingdom. The reign sung in 19:6 begins after 19:19-21.

The marriage of the Lamb is associated in the prophetic hymn with the beginning of the kingdom and the coming of the conquering Christ. *It has not yet occurred.* It did not occur at a supposed rapture at an earlier time. The actual union of the bride and Groom is not even pictured; only the announcement of it is given. As the hymn proclaims the future beginning of the kingdom, it proclaims the future marriage feast; but both are in the immediate future, and both take place after Christ returns.

The full force of the prophetic character of this vision may be felt by referring again to the visions of chapter 14. *In vision,* John sees the 144,000 standing on Mount Zion. In vision, the millennium has begun, Christ has returned, and the 144,000 have entered into their millennial reign. They "follow the Lamb whithersoever he goeth," and when He reigns on earth, they share His reign. *The reality which is seen in vision does not occur until chapter 20.*

So the vision of the bride prepared for the wedding feast is prophetic. *In vision,* John sees the bride ready for the marriage; but this is not a vision depicting either the saints in the intermediate state or the Church in heaven prior to the return of Christ. It is a vision of what shall be after Christ returns. Then will occur the resurrection of the dead in Christ, both saints and martyrs (20:4). The final proof that this is a prophetic vision is the fact that the dead in Christ are not yet raised; their resurrection occurs after the return of Christ (20:4).

In the Revelation, there is only one coming of Christ, and it takes place at the end of the Tribulation. It has a two-fold significance. To the Church, it means a banquet of joy, the marriage supper of the Lamb (19:9); to the world, it means a banquet of death (19:17-18), a visitation of judgment. Christ is both the Blessed Groom and Conquering King.

The Necessity of an Interval

We would append to this chapter a brief word about a common argument used for separating the Rapture from the Revelation. It is frequently said that since the saints must appear before the judgment seat of Christ to receive rewards for the things done in the body before they come to earth with Him, there must of necessity be an interval of time between the Rapture and the Revelation for this judgment to take place.

To this, two questions must be raised. First, where does the Word of God say that the saints are to be rewarded before Christ returns in glory? What is there to prevent this judgment of rewards from taking place after Christ has come in victory and established His millennial kingdom? In the millennium, the saints are to reign with Him, and perhaps the first period of the millennial reign will be devoted to the apportioning of kingly authority on the basis of the faithfulness manifested in earthly existence. Something like this may be involved in the parable of the pounds in Luke 19:11-19.

Secondly, if a period of time must intervene for this judgment to take place, will seven years be enough? It is estimated that there are two hundred million living Christians. In seven years, there are just over two hundred million *seconds*. How much of a fraction of a second is necessary for the judgment of each believer? If an interval of time is needed, then far more than seven years will be required.

Summary

We have now examined closely the main bases within Scripture upon which pretribulationism rests. We have found that in each instance, the Biblical data require interpretation. Nowhere is a pretribulation rapture asserted. Furthermore, in *no instance are the facts such that they require the theory of a pretribulation rapture.* Theoretically, it is possible that such expressions as Christ's coming for His saints and with His saints, the day of Christ and the day of the Lord could refer to two different events. However, we have examined the Scriptures closely and have found other interpretations which are at least equally possible and valid. Therefore, pretribulationism is an unnecessary inference. It is an assumption in light of which the Scriptures are interpreted. Nowhere can its adherents really say, "Thus saith the Lord." Students of the Word may be permitted to make such an inference if they care to do so, but in such an important matter, they should be willing to admit that it is an assumption and not the sure Word of God; and that another inference, viz., that of a single coming of Christ to rapture the Church at the close of the Tribulation has an equal if not a stronger claim to support.

6

WATCH

THERE ARE other reasons which are used to support the idea of a pretribulation rapture. One of the most persuasive and most frequently repeated arguments is that which rests upon the frequent exhortations of the Scripture for believers to watch. In view of the repeated exhortations for Christ's coming, His return must be imminent, and therefore it must occur before the Great Tribulation. It is said that it is impossible to watch for something which cannot occur for a fixed interval of time. If for instance, I know that my friend is to visit me but I know he is not coming until some time next week after a certain convention which he is attending is over, I will not watch for him to come today or tomorrow. I will not watch until the convention is over and the time for his visit has come.

If Christ's coming is to occur only after the Great Tribulation has run its course, it would be impossible for me today to watch for the Lord's return, for I know He will not come today. He will not return until the Tribulation has taken place. The command to watch, therefore, could have relevance only for tribulation saints and could not be directed to the Church throughout the centuries. Yet we are told to watch. We can watch for His coming only if it is imminent. Imminence means that no prophesied event stands in the way and must be fulfilled before the return of Christ. Therefore the next event on the prophetic calendar after Christ's ascension must be His return to rapture the Church. It can occur at any moment; it must therefore precede the Tribulation. Thus the Church is destined to be raptured before the Tribulation takes place.

This line of reasoning appears to be very persuasive; but all such questions must be answered by an appeal to the Word of God. What does the Scripture really teach? Does it teach that we are to watch for an event which can take place at any moment.

There are five different words in the New Testament which are translated by our English word "watch." Two of these words, *tereo* and *paratereo* bear the meaning of "watching" in the sense of keeping the attention focused upon the object of concern. The soldiers at the cross were there for the purpose of keeping watch over Jesus (Matt. 27:36, 54). The Pharisees watched Jesus to see if he would perform a miracle on the Sabbath (Mk. 3:2; Lk. 6:7; see also Lk. 14:1; 20:20). The Jews watched the gates at Damascus that they might apprehend Paul when he attempted to leave the city (Acts 9:24). *These words which refer to the physical act of fixing one's attention upon some object are never used of the second coming of Christ.*

Another word is *nepho*. In I Peter 4:7, this word is translated in our Authorized Version as follows: "But the end of all things is at hand: be ye therefore sober, and *watch* unto prayer." This word, however, which is here translated by the word "watch," literally means "to be sober." The Revised Version of 1900 renders this verse "Be ye therefore of sound mind, and be *sober* unto prayer." In I Peter 1:13, even our Authorized Version translates the word "be sober" in view of the hope of the revelation of Jesus: "be sober, and hope to the end for the grace that is to be brought to you at the revelation of Jesus Christ." *Nepho* does not mean "to watch" but to have a sober mind and character.

The two words commonly used to admonish watchfulness with relation to the Lord's return are *gregoreo* and *agrupneo*. And they have a similar meaning. *Agrupneo* means "to be sleepless" or "wakeful," and thus "to be vigilant." The noun, *agrupnia*, occurs only twice in the New Testament where it is used to refer to loss of sleep and to wakeful nights (II Cor. 6:5; 11:27). The verb is used of general spiritual vigilance in Ephesians 6:18, and in Hebrews 13:17; it refers to the vigilance of Christian leaders over their flock.

The verb is used only twice in connection with the end of the age. "Take ye heed, watch and pray: for you know not when the time is" (Mk. 13:33). We shall discuss this verse below when we study this entire passage. The other use is in Luke 21:36: "But watch ye at every season, making supplication, that ye may prevail to escape all these things that shall come to pass, and to stand before the Son of man." This verse was treated in the preceding chapter, where we found that "these things" which the believer is to escape are "the things which are coming on the world" in verse 26, viz., the divine judgments of the end from which the believer will be sheltered. These will occur in the last part of the Great Tribulation. This verse cannot teach a pretribulation rapture for it is addressed to people who find themselves in the midst of that Tribulation. Furthermore, the command to watch does not mean "to look for" but "to be wakeful." Those who are spiritually asleep, i.e., the worldly, the ungodly, will be caught in judgment as in a snare. Those who are spiritually awake, God's people, will escape judgment and will stand before the Son of man; i.e., they will be given the joy of entering into His presence and fellowship at His coming. There is no hint of watching for a secret coming of Christ in this passage.

The word *gregoreo* means "to be awake." In the deep shadows of the Garden of Gethsemane, when Jesus' soul was agonizing in the face of the cross, He longed for His closest disciples to "watch" with Him, that is, to join Him in His spiritual watch and in the exercise of prayer (Matt. 26:38,40,41). In I Thessalonians 5:10, the word means "to be alive" in contrast to the sleep of death. In a number of places, the word is used of general spiritual alertness. Paul exhorted the Ephesian elders to watchfulness (Acts 20:31). To the Corinthians he wrote, "Watch ye, stand fast in the faith" (I Cor. 16:13). The Colossians are exhorted to "continue stedfastly in prayer, watching therein with thanksgiving" (Col. 4:2). Peter exhorts to sobriety and watchfulness in view of the fierceness of the hostility of the adversary the Devil, who goes about as a roaring lion seeking whom he may devour (I Pet. 5:8). The exhortation in Revelation 3:2,3 to the church in Sardis to watch does not mean that they were neglecting the doctrine of the Lord's return. The word refers to their spiritual lethargy and their dead condition. Williams correctly translates the passage "wake up, and strengthen what is left, although it is on the very point of dying . . . . If you do not wake up, I will come like a thief, and you will never know the hour when I came unto you" (Rev. 3:2,3). Verkuyl translates it, "In case you do not keep wide awake, I will come upon you like a thief." The "coming" of Christ to the church in Sardis does not refer to His glorious second advent but to a visitation in judgment. This is recognized by the Scofield Bible which has no marginal reference associating this verse with the second advent.

In all of these verses, *gregoreo* is used of general spiritual vigilance without immediate reference to the second coming of Christ. There remain nine uses of the word in which God's people are exhorted to watch in view of the impending end.

Can a doctrine of an any-moment rapture of the Church and a sudden unexpected coming of Christ be built upon these verses? Only two of these exhortations occur outside of our Lord's teachings. Only once does Paul specifically exhort believers to watch in view of Christ's return. He had taught the Thessalonians the blessed truth of the resurrection of the dead and the Rapture of the Church at the return of Christ. As to the time of Christ's return and the Rapture, Paul says that it will come unexpectedly. When men say "Peace and safety, then sudden destruction cometh upon them, as travail upon a woman with child; and they shall in no wise escape." Then Paul adds, "But ye brethren, are not in darkness, that that day should overtake you as a thief; for ye are all sons of light, and sons of the day: we are not of the night, nor of darkness; so then let us not sleep, as do the rest, but let us watch and be sober" (I Thess. 5:3-5).

Two observations are necessary. First, watching is required not in view of the Rapture of the Church, but in view of the day of the Lord, which according to the dispensational outline comes at the end of the Tribulation. This command to watch, therefore, cannot be used to prove an any-moment unexpected coming of Christ for which the believer is to watch, for the day of the Lord will come only after definite signs such as the Antichrist and the apostasy which will indicate to those who are watching that the end is near.

It is very easy in these things to confuse apparently logical inference with the explicit teaching of the Word. For instance, a current article in a prophetic journal asserts that the commands to look for Christ's return are "exhortations which would be meaningless unless that event is an ever-present possibility." The writer then quotes several proof-texts to support his statement and adds, "None of these Scriptures is capable of misunderstanding, if it be taken at face value." But the first proof-text is Titus 2:13, "looking for the blessed hope and appearing (epiphany) of the glory of our great God and Saviour Jesus Christ." We ought to take this verse at its "face-value," and when we do, we find that we are to look not for a secret coming of Christ before the Tribulation, but for the glorious epiphany of Christ which admittedly occurs at the end of the Tribulation. This verse is, we agree, quite incapable of misunderstanding, but it is incapable of supporting the teaching of watching for a pretribulation, secret coming of Christ. The epiphany of Christ cannot occur at any moment. It can occur in our generation but only after the Tribulation has run its course. Yet the Word of God commands us to look for this glorious event. This is surely no meaningless exhortation.

Secondly, the exhortation to watch is a warning lest the coming of Christ be an event which will catch believers unprepared. The fact is that Christ's coming will not be unexpected to those who are watching. To them, it will not come as a thief, for those who belong to Christ will not be asleep but will be sober and watching. It is clear that unexpectedness of that day "like a thief" has its application to those who are not Christians. To those who are not watching, who are saying, "Peace and safety," the day will come like a thief and will bring sudden destruction. To those who are watching the day will be no surprise. It is equally clear that the "watching" enjoined does not refer to fixing the attention upon some event which is likely to occur at any moment. The context makes it clear that the "watch" means *to be spiritually awake* in contrast to the world which is slumbering in the sleep of sin. "For they that sleep sleep in the night; and they that are drunken are drunken in the night. But let us, since we are of the day, be sober" (I Thess. 5:7,8). Williams again correctly translates the word "watch" in this passage: "So let us stop sleeping as others do, but let us stay awake and keep sober." If there is any teaching of a sudden unexpected coming of Christ in this passage, it refers to the world. Paul explicitly says that believers will not be taken unexpectedly, not because they are looking for the coming of Christ to take place at any moment, but because they are awake whenever it occurs.

An exhortation to watchfulness is found in Revelation 16:15, connected with the outpouring of the sixth bowl, an event which brings us to the very end of the Great Tribulation immediately preceding the glorious return of Christ with His saints. "Behold, I come as a thief. Blessed is he that watcheth, and keepeth his garments, lest he walk naked, and they see his shame." If Christ's coming "as a thief" means a coming which is entirely unexpected, without any preceding signs, this verse should never have been written. At the pouring out of the sixth vial, we are at the end of the period when according to uniform pretribulation teaching, the seventieth week of Daniel is drawing to its close. In the middle of the week, Antichrist has broken his covenant with the nation Israel and has launched upon a fearful persecution of the restored Jewish nation. God will then pour out the vials of His wrath upon the Beast and the worshippers of the Beast. In such a day, any believers who on the earth, whether they be within the Jewish restoration or the circle of Gentile believers, by turning to the Word of God could know almost the precise time of Christ's return at the end of the three and a half years. However, they are exhorted to watch, because Christ is coming as a thief. Whatever this means, it cannot involve a secret, any-moment, unexpected return of Christ. The exhortation obviously is to spiritual wakefulness, and is similar to Paul's exhortation just discussed.

There remain eight uses of the word in our Lord's teachings concerning the end of the age and His return. The word is used twice in Luke 12:37,39 where it is practically parallel to Matthew 24:43ff. Five times in the Olivet Discourse, Jesus exhorts to watchfulness; and here the exhortation is distinctly associated with the uncertainty of the time of the end. The passages need to be studied, in a harmony of the Gospels, because there is some overlapping. We shall quote from Mark and Matthew, arranging the material in the order in which it appears in a harmony.

"Take ye heed, watch (*agrupneo*) and pray: for ye know not when the time is. It is as when a man, sojourning in another country, having left his house and given authority to his servants, to each one his work, commanded also the porter to watch (*gregoreo*). Watch therefore: for ye know not when the Lord of the house cometh, whether at even, or at midnight, or at cock crowing, or in the morning; lest coming suddenly he find you sleeping.

And what I say unto you I say unto all, watch" (Mk. 13:33-37). "But know this, that if the master of the house had known in what watch the thief was coming, he would have watched, and would not have suffered his house to be broken through. Therefore be ye also ready; for in an hour that ye think not the Son of man cometh" (Matt. 24:42-44). These verses set before us, along with the parallel passages in Luke 12:37, 39, and Matthew 24:42 every exhortation which Jesus made to "watch" because of the uncertainty of the end.

Let us admit at the outset that if we take these verses out of their setting and read them superficially, they give the impression that the event described is to take place without any warnings or signs to indicate that it is near, and in view of its utter unexpectedness, men are exhorted to watch. It is this impression which is gained from a casual reading that the verses have been interpreted to teach an any-moment coming of Christ. We must, however, study every command in the Word of God within its own context. When this is done, it becomes immediately apparent that no teaching of an any-moment rapture of the Church and an unexpected secret coming of Christ can be built upon these exhortations. For the fact is, *all of these exhortations have reference to the glorious appearing of the Son of man at the end of the Tribulation.*

The main structure of the Olivet Discourse is quite clear. Matthew 24:4-14 describes the character of the age down to its end. Verses 15-28 describe the fearful events which will immediately attend the consummation of the age. They consist of three events: the Antichrist (v. 15), the Great Tribulation (vv. 16-26), and the glorious coming of Christ (vv. 27, 28). The following paragraph (vv. 29-31) enlarges upon verse 27 to describe in greater detail the revelation of Christ when He shall come on the clouds of heaven with power and great glory. The rest of the chapter which contains the passages we are discussing gives the spiritual application, the main thrust of which is to watchfulness.

For what are we to watch? For a secret coming of Christ? No such coming is mentioned or even intimated in the entire chapter. The only coming of Christ which is suggested is His glorious Revelation which takes place at the end of the Great Tribulation. Are we to watch for a secret rapture of the Church? The only verse in the chapter which can possibly refer to a rapture is verse 31, when the Son of man sends forth His angels with the sound of a trumpet to gather His elect from the four winds, from one end of heaven to the other. But if this is the Rapture, it occurs at the end of the Tribulation, and therefore is an event whose time can be approximately understood. Therefore, most Bible teachers who hold to an any-moment rapture of the Church and a secret coming of Christ are forced to conclude that these doctrines are not revealed in the Olivet Discourse. We are told that the Rapture of the Church is a mystery which was revealed for the first time to Paul and is found nowhere in the Gospels.

Then are we to conclude that Jesus exhorted believers to watch for an event about which He said absolutely nothing? Would He exhort them to watch for an event which He does not mention and which does not appear upon the horizon of His instruction? Such a procedure empties the exhortation to watch of its significance. I cannot watch for something of which I have no knowledge; and certainly Jesus did not teach men to watch for something about which He did not instruct them.

Some Bible teachers who hold a pretribulation rapture have felt the force of this argument and therefore have applied the commands of our Lord to watch in Matthew 24 to the Jewish remnant in the Tribulation. A. C. Gaebelein, interpreting the meaning of verses 43 and 44 says, "with these words of warning and exhortation to watch, our Lord closes the predictions relating to the end of the Jewish age. This warning will be understood and heeded by the Jewish remnant, to which it is addressed. They are to *watch* for the Son of man; the church is to *wait* for the Lord" (*The*

Gospel of Matthew, Vol. II, p. 217). One of the most recent statements of a pretribulation rapture applies these verses in the same way. After quoting Matthew 24:37-42, English says, "The same circumstances that attended the time just prior to the judgment of the flood will pertain before the return of Christ in judgment upon the world. Business will be going on as usual. People will be occupied with the normal duties of life. . . . Then suddenly the Lord will come. . . . The allusion is most certainly to the time of the coming of the Son of man in power and glory. That coming is unquestionably after the tribulation. . . . This passage cannot be used as a proof text that the church will pass through the tribulation. It has to do with those who are on earth when Christ returns to earth — those taken will be those who have rejected God and his Christ; those left will be tribulation saints, Israel primarily, who will enter the earthly kingdom" (*Rethinking the Rapture,* pp. 49, 50).

Such admissions as these are fatal to the theory of an any-moment rapture and a secret coming of Christ which is based on the argument that the exhortations to watch require such an any-moment return of Christ. If pretribulationists can apply these words without difficulty to the Jewish remnant in the Tribulation and yet admit that they are exhorted to watch for an event which will take place at the end of the seventieth week, although they "do not know the day or the hour," then two results inevitably follow. First, if the exhortations do belong to the Jewish remnant, they do not apply to the Church. Jesus then did not exhort the Church to watch for an unexpected event. In this case, there does not appear either in the Gospels or in the Epistles or in the Revelation a teaching that the Church is to watch for a sudden, any-moment coming of Christ.

Secondly, if pretribulationists can apply the command to watch to *anyone* in the midst of the Tribulation whose end can be approximately known, then they cannot object to the application of these same exhortations to the Church *on the ground* that it is impossible for believers to watch for an event whose time can be approximately known. If the Jews can be told to "watch" for an event which will take place three and a half years after Antichrist breaks covenant with them, then Christians can be told to watch for an event which will not take place until the end of the Great Tribulation. In either case, it is impossible to build the teaching of a secret, any-moment coming of Christ to rapture the Church on these exhortations.

The entire argument that the exhortations to watch require an any-moment coming of Christ is based on a misunderstanding. The true meaning of the command to watch is not to watch *for* Christ's return. Scripture does not use this language. *Nowhere are we told to watch for the coming of Christ.* We are exhorted, rather, in view of the uncertainty of the time of the end, to watch. "Watching" does not mean "looking for" the event; it means spiritual and moral "wakefulness." We do not know when the end will come. Therefore, whenever it happens, we must be spiritually awake and must not sleep. If we are awake and Christ comes today, we are ready. If we are awake and Christ does not come until tomorrow, we will still be ready. Whenever it happens, we must be ready.

There remain warnings to watch which are combined with the idea of looking for Christ's return; and these are found outside of the Olivet Discourse and provide the strongest basis for the idea of watching for an any-moment event.

In Luke 12:22-24, Jesus exhorted the disciples against becoming inextricably involved in the cares and concerns of earthly existence so that the true character of their life is lost. These sayings are parallel to those in the Sermon on the Mount. The disciple is not to find his treasure on earth but in heaven (vs. 34), for present existence is transitory; he is to live all his life in expectation of the return of Christ which will bring the present state of existence to its end. The believer is living for the life of the age to come. Therefore, life is to be characterized by an attitude of expectancy toward the attainment of that life. We are to be *looking for* Christ's return. "Be ye yourselves like unto men looking for their lord" (vs. 36).

The use of the word "looking for" does not carry with it the necessary idea of an any-moment event, although it does connote a *complex of events* which might begin at any time. We may discover the meaning of the word from its uses elsewhere. Simeon was a righteous and devout man who was "looking for the consolation of Israel" (Luke 2:25). Joseph of Arimathea was "looking for the kingdom of God" (Luke 23:51). Both of these pious Jews were living in constant expectation of a complex of events which would include the appearing of Messiah, the over-throw of the enemies of God, and the inauguration of the kingdom of God — events which we now know include the totality of all that is involved in *both* advents of Christ.

This may provide the clue for the understanding of our Lord's admonitions. S. P. Tregelles has pointed out that Jesus employed a metaphor to describe His return in which a sign preceded the actual event. "Be ye yourselves like unto men looking for their lord, when he shall return from the marriage feast; that, when he cometh and knocketh, they may straightway open unto him." (vs. 36). The hope of Christ's coming does not exclude that His knock shall first be heard. His actual coming is preceded by this signal which indicates that He is at the door.

The interpretation of this passage in the interests of an any-moment coming of the Lord overlooks its main thrust. The reason for the exhortation to watch is not so much that Christ may come at any moment as it is that He may not come for some time. The central problem is the delay of the parousia. His return may not be until the second watch, or even the third watch, late into the night. The point of the warning is that we cannot say it will be soon; we do not know when. Therefore, we must be always ready, for we do not know when He will come.

It is because of the *uncertainty* of the time, not its imminence, that we are to watch; and the idea again is of wakefulness rather than concentration of attention. The servants are always to be *awake* that they may be ready to open to the master and serve his needs (vs. 37). This thought is further developed in the next paragraph. Watching is defined not so much as an attitude as a conduct. "Blessed is that servant, whom his lord when he cometh shall find *so doing*" (vs. 43). Jesus Himself suggests that there will be delay (vs. 45); the important thing is what is done with the interval during which the Lord delays His return. He who "watches" is the faithful and wise steward (vs. 42), who is busy in his master's service. He who does not watch is the steward who begins to beat the servants, and to become drunk (vs. 45-6). "Watching" then means faithfulness in service. It means spiritual awakeness.

Furthermore, the difference between those who watch and those who do not is not between two classes of Christians — those who are worldly and separated, but between two classes of professing Christians — true servants and false servants. This is seen in the punishment meted out to those who did not watch: they are cut asunder and punished with the unfaithful (vs. 46). *The delay of the master made no difference to the true servant;* he busied himself about his Lord's business. He was continually watching. But the master's delay induced the false servant to a sinful course of action. *The Lord's delay brought out the true character of his servants*: whether they were truly his servants or only professing to be servants when in reality they had no affection for their master.

If we apply this line of reasoning to our present situation, a rather unexpected conclusion emerges. We must conclude that we ought not to need an any-moment coming of Christ as a necessary incentive to faithfulness in service and conduct. The true motive is a heart devotion, and even though Christ tarries, the true servant will always

watch; he will never lapse into the state of spiritual som-
nambulance and moral laxity.

Again, the unexpectedness of the Lord's coming is directed primarily to the faithless servants. It is of the steward
who, in light of the lord's delay, begins to beat the servants
and to get drunk that Jesus said, "the lord of that servant
shall come in a day when he expecteth not, and in an hour
when he knoweth not, and shall cut him asunder, and ap-
point his portion with the unfaithful" (vs. 46). This is the
further elaboration of the saying in verse 40, "Be ye also
ready, for in an hour that ye think not the Son of man
cometh."

Finally, and most conclusively, the coming of the Son of
man for which we are to be ready is not the secret coming
of Christ at the beginning of the Tribulation to rapture the
Church. It is the event described in Matthew 24:27 and
30, the glorious appearing of the Son of man on the clouds
of heaven at the close of the Tribulation. This is the only
aspect of Christ's coming taught in the synoptic Gospels. If
then, all of the exhortations to watch in the Gospels are related to the Revelation of Christ at the end of the Tribulation, it is obviously impossible to base an any-moment
coming of Christ on the exhortations to watch for this
event; for in the pretribulationist outline, this event will be
preceded by the Antichrist and the Great Tribulation.

We have now surveyed all of the references in the New
Testament where the Spirit exhorts us to watch. Nowhere
are we told to watch for a secret, any-moment coming of
Christ to rapture the Church. The commands to watch
mean to be spiritually awake, to be ready to meet the Lord
whenever He comes. The exhortations to watch in the
Gospels are all addressed to people who will be looking for
the glorious appearing of Christ at the end of the Tribulation.

The argument therefore that the Biblical teaching to
watch demands an any-moment coming of Christ and
therefore a pretribulation rapture is not well grounded. It

is an apparently logical inference, an interpretation which seems very persuasive; but when we turn from the assumption of this interpretation to examine carefully what the Word of God actually says, we find no assertion of an any-moment coming for which we are to watch. We are indeed to be ready for the coming of Christ, for we do not know when the Lord will come. Therefore we must always be awake. Even though His coming is delayed, we must be awake so that His return will be no surprise.

7

WRATH OR TRIBULATION?

THERE IS another reason used by pretribulationists to support their position which is equally persuasive and widely used. It is the argument that God never confuses His judgments. The Great Tribulation will see the outpouring of God's wrath upon the world; and it is inconceivable that God will permit His Church — those redeemed by the blood of the Lamb, His bride — to suffer the judgments of the Great Tribulation, which are a manifestation of the wrath of God against a sinful and rebellious civilization (Rev. 15:1). Therefore we must infer that the Church is to be taken out of the world before the Tribulation begins.

We have already pointed out that it is a clear teaching of Scripture that the Church will never suffer the wrath of God. At this point we are in agreement with pretribulationists. If the position rested upon this one fact alone, pretribulationism would be inevitable.

There are however two alternatives to that of a pretribulation rapture. One is that the Church will be raptured toward the end of the Tribulation just before God pours out His wrath upon unbelieving men. This view is usuallly called midtribulationism, for it holds that the Church will be raptured somewhere in the midst of the period of Tribulation.

This view was suggested by Dr. Harold John Ockenga, Pastor of Park Street Church in Boston, in a recent article in *Christian Life* (February, 1955). Ockenga correctly distinguishes between tribulation and wrath, and suggests that the Church will be taken out of the world just before the period of the wrath of God at the very end of the Tribulation. Ockenga apparently classes himself with those who believe "the church will suffer man's wrath but not God's wrath."

Dr. J. Oliver Buswell, Jr., formerly president of Wheaton and Shelton Colleges also rejects the usual pretribulation rapture in favor of midtribulationism. "I do not believe that the Church will go through any part of that period which the Scripture specifically designates as the wrath of God, but I do believe that the abomination of desolation will be a specific signal for a hasty flight followed by a very brief but a very terrible persecution, and that followed very quickly by the rapture of the Church *preceding* the outpouring of the vials of the wrath of God" (*Our Hope*, June, 1950).

It should be pointed out that such a midtribulation view as that suggested by Buswell and Ockenga destroys the usual "any-moment" view of Christ's coming. The Lord will not return, according to this interpetation, until Antichrist appears and the Great Tribulation comes upon the world and the Church. No one can expect the Lord to come at any moment until he finds himself well in the midst of the Great Tribulation.

Midtribulationism however is faced with the same exegetical problems which confront pretribulationism. The Scripture nowhere asserts that the Rapture will take place at the beginning of the period of wrath. Furthermore, it is difficult to determine the temporal limits of this period if it is not the last three and a half years.

There is a second alternative. It is possible, and we believe that the Scriptures indicate, that the Church will be on earth throughout the entire period of the Tribulation but will be divinely sheltered from the wrath of God.

As Dr. Ockenga pointed out in the article mentioned above, pretribulationists are in error in identifying tribulation and wrath. The Great Tribulation will consist of these two elements: tribulation at the hands of Antichrist, and the wrath of God. These two are not to be confused. Since this is important for a solution to this problem, we must survey the New Testament teaching about tribulation and wrath.

Everyone must agree that it is inconceivable that the Church will suffer the wrath of God. The Word of God is very clear in its teaching that those who have found salvation through the shed blood of Christ are thereby forever delivered from the wrath of God which is revealed from heaven against all unrighteousness and ungodliness of men (Rom. 1:18). The wrath of God rests only upon the one who refuses to believe in the Lord Jesus Christ (Jn. 3:36). God in the kindness of His love would turn men unto repentance, but men who persist in the way of impenitence and who harden their hearts against the kindness of God store up wrath for themselves on the day of wrath when God's righteous judgment will be revealed (Rom. 2:5). However, those who have turned in penitence for their sins to repose faith in Christ are now justified by His blood and shall be saved by him from the wrath of God (Rom. 5:9). We who were once children of wrath are now the children of a loving God (Eph. 2:3). In the day of judgment, the wrath of God will come upon the sons of disobedience, not upon those who have become the sons of God (Eph. 5:6). Those who believe in Jesus and are living in expectation of His glorious return shall be delivered from the wrath to come (I Thess. 1:10) which shall be inflicted upon those who do not know God and who do not obey the Gospel of the Lord Jesus (II Thess. 1:8). God has not destined His people to wrath but to obtain salvation through our Lord Jesus Christ (I Thess. 5:9). Such verses refer primarily to God's wrath in the final judgment. But the Great Tribulation will in one of its aspects be the outpouring of the divine wrath upon a rebellious and sinful civilization. It is the out-reaching of final judgment just before the end comes. It is in fact the beginning of that judgment.

The book of Revelation is the book of consummations. The consummation is effected in three different directions. There must be in the first place the consummation of the salvation of God's people. At the very heart of salvation in the book of Revelation is the cross of Christ; for it is a Lamb bearing the marks of slaughter and sacrifice who stands at the throne of God who is the key to the whole book (Rev. 5:6). What Christ has accomplished on His cross is a finished work, but the salvation of God's people is not complete and will not be brought to consummation apart from the glorious return of Christ. The state of the martyrs seen at the opening of the fifth seal (Rev. 6:9-11) is not one in which they are enjoying the full blessings of the final consummation. They are indeed enjoying a rest of blessedness, but it is not one in which they have entered into the enjoyment of perfect final bliss. They are admonished rather to rest a little longer until the time of full consummation has arrived. Perfect blessedness will be enjoyed only after the marriage supper of the Lamb (Rev. 19:9). And this awaits the glorious return of Christ.

A second line of consummation is seen in the evil character of human civilization. The entire New Testament agrees in the portrait of an age which is dominated by evil powers and which will never become the scene of the full realization of God's kingdom until Christ Himself has returned to transform this age into the age to come. There is no room in the Biblical portrait either for a postmillennial scheme of a perfect conquest of the world through the preaching of the Gospel until this age becomes the scene of God's perfect kingdom, or for idealistic schemes of social amelioration which interpret the mission of the Church in terms of social action. The character of this age is evil (Gal. 1:4). Satan is called the god of this age (II Cor. 4:4). While indeed the children of God are the light of the world and the salt of the earth (Matt. 5:13, 14) and must inevitably exercise a salutary influence for righteousness and godliness upon the society of which they are a part, the Word of God makes it very clear that it is not within the purpose of God by such means to accomplish the complete salvation of this age. On the contrary, evil is seen to be like a vineyard which is ripening until the harvest is necessary (Rev. 14:17-20). The rise of Antichrist at the end of the age will be the embodiment in its most concentrated form of the powers of evil which have been operative throughout the course of human history. When evil has come to its fruition, Christ will then appear in judgment.

The third line of consummation is that of divine judgment. God's judgments against evil have been operating throughout the course of human history. The fall of Jerusalem and the destruction of the Jewish state was a manifestation of God's judgment in righteous wrath against a nation which had rejected their Messiah. It is in anticipation of this historical judgment that Paul asserts that God's wrath has come upon Israel in full measure (I Thess. 2:16).

All the Scriptures point to a day when the wrath of God will find its fullest manifestation in a supernatural manifestation which will issue in the final condemnation and just punishment of all wickedness and evil. The second coming of Christ to a godless civilization will mean a visitation of wrath. The sixth seal (Rev. 6:12-17) gives a brief anticipation of this day when men of every social and economic status will flee and seek to hide "from the face of him that sitteth on the throne, and from the wrath of the Lamb; for the great day of their wrath is come, and who is able to stand?" The representation of the second coming of Christ in Revelation 19:11-16 places its primary emphasis upon His coming in judgment. His robe which is dipped in blood (v. 13) is not sprinkled with His own blood shed on the cross but is stained in blood as though He had been engaged in victorious battle. In this visitation, "he treadeth the winepress of the fierceness of the wrath of God, the Almighty" (v. 15).

Against this background we may understand that one aspect of the Great Tribulation is the beginning of this outpouring of wrath. Immediately preceding the victorious return of Christ, great supernatural events will take place which will embody the beginnings of the visitation of wrath upon a godless and corrupted society. At the sounding of the seventh trumpet, the twenty-four elders offered a song of thanksgiving unto God because He is at the point of assuming His power and inaugurating the fullness of His reign upon the earth. This involves the visitation of wrath upon the world (Rev. 11:17,18). The plagues which were involved in the sounding of the seven trumpets and the outpouring of the seven bowls may be thought of as the beginning of the day of judgment. By these plagues, God is manifesting His holy wrath and warning men that the day of final judgment is beginning. But this has a merciful purpose; there remains a final moment of time. Repentance is still possible. It is implied in Revelation 9:20 that these visitations were designed to be a warning to men and to lead them to repentance from their idolatry and their wickedness. This basically merciful purpose in the preliminary outpourings of God's wrath is again suggested in Revelation 16:8 at the outpouring of the fourth bowl.

Now it is quite clear that it is contradictory to the character of the divine purpose to inflict these woes upon God's own people. And this again we would assert: the Church will certainly not experience these outpourings of the wrath of God. The seven bowls of the wrath of God are designed not for the world at large but for "the men who bore the mark of the beast and worshipped its image" (Rev. 16:2). In preparation for the seven bowls, an angel cried with a loud voice, "If any man worshippeth the beast and his image, and receiveth a mark on his forehead or upon his hand, he also shall drink the wine of the wrath of God, which is prepared unmixed in the cup of his anger" (Rev. 14:9).

During the Tribulation, a company of 144,000 are seen on earth who have been sealed with the seal of the living

God, the specific purpose of which is to protect its recipients from participation in the sufferings imposed by the last plagues of God's wrath. This appears in the sounding of the fifth trumpet, for the plague which follows is directed specifically against "such men as have not the seal of God on their foreheads" (Rev. 9:4).

The identity of this sealed and protected group is disputed by interpreters of the Revelation. Some insist that they are literal, racial Jews, for they are derived from each of the twelve tribes of Israel. Others insist that they cannot be literal Jews for the twelve tribes by which they are described are not the twelve tribes of Israel. It is a fact that these twelve tribes nowhere appear in the Old Testament in any of the listings of the twelve tribes of Israel. Dan is omitted, yet according to Ezekiel 48:1, Dan is to have his portion in the land. How then can these twelve tribes be literal Jews since they are not the literal twelve tribes of Israel?

Furthermore, we must note that the Apocalypse specifically distinguishes between true and false Jews, i.e., between those who are Jews literally but not spiritually (2:9, 3:9). It is possible therefore that by the 144,000 from twelve tribes, the Spirit of God means to suggest that the true Israel, the true people of God will be preserved absolutely complete. Not one person who really belongs to the true Israel will be lost, even in the Great Tribulation.

However, whether literal or spiritual Israel, one fact is clear: God will protect His people from the outpourings of wrath in the Great Tribulation, whether they are Jews or Gentiles. Whoever they are, we are assured that the people of God, even though they are living on the earth during these last terrible days, will be sealed by God that they may be protected and sheltered from the experience of the outpouring of wrath which will be directed against those who are worshipping and following the beast. We are therefore in essential agreement at this point with those who teach a rapture of the Church before the Tribulation, that the Church will not experience the wrath of God. God protected the children of Israel in Egypt; and as the sign of the blood over the doorway spared every Israelite family from the loss of the firstborn son, so will God's people be spared from the supernatural visitation embodied in the outpouring of the wrath of God at the end of the age, be they Jews or Gentiles.

This protection from the wrath of God, however, is not identical with deliverance from the wrath of the Beast. It would be contrary to the entire history of God's dealings with His people both in the Old and New Testament dispensations if God should in the consummation of the age reverse Himself to do something He has never previously done, namely, to protect His people from the hostility of an evil age. Israel was permitted to groan in slavery for many years under the harsh hand of Egypt. First Assyria and then Babylon were used as divine agencies to discipline Israel and in the process, the people of God were reduced to an abject state of servitude. In the intertestamental period, the Jews experienced the most fearful persecution of their history at the hands of Antiochus Epiphanes, a persecution which is predicted in the eighth chapter of the prophecy of Daniel. Here for the first time in history, the hostility of Satan was directed toward the objective of the complete obliteration of the worship of God, and it is for this reason that this persecution is included in the prophecies of Daniel. Indeed the objectives of Antiochus were of such a character that he becomes a type of the last persecuting enemy of God's people, Antichrist himself.

Throughout the history of the Christian Church, God has permitted His people to suffer again and again at the hands of civil governments and rulers who were hostile to the things of God and therefore became instruments in the hands of the prince of evil. Jesus Himself prophesied that throughout the course of the age, His disciples would experience tribulation and death; they would be hated by all nations for His name's sake (Matt. 24:9). Because of

the character of the age, Jesus promised that in the world
His disciples would have tribulation (Jn. 16:33). It is indeed the divine order that "through many tribulations it is
necessary for us to enter into the kingdom of God" (Acts
14:22). The Christians in Thessalonica received the Gospel accompanied by much tribulation (I Thess. 1:6), an
experience which Paul assures them is destined to be their
lot. "For when we were with you, we told you beforehand
that we were to suffer tribulation; just as it has now come
to pass, and as you know" (I Thess. 3:4). Indeed, Paul assured the Thessalonians that they may expect deliverance
from tribulation only at the revelation of the Lord Jesus
with His mighty angels when He comes to inflict judgment
upon those who have afflicted His people with tribulation
(II Thess. 1:5-8). It must be pointed out to those who
teach that the coming of Christ is to be twofold, a secret
coming to rapture the Church at the beginning of the Tribulation and a public manifestation in divine judgment at
the end of the Tribulation, that the promise of deliverance
in this passage does not point to the Rapture of the Church,
but to the day of the Lord when He is gloriously manifested in judgment. Until that day comes, tribulation may
be expected.

It is furthermore to be noted that in all of the verses
which we have cited, the word which is used in the Greek
New Testament is *thlipsis*, though it is variously translated
in our English versions. This is the same word used in
Matthew 24:21 to refer to the Great Tribulation. The final
Tribulation will be the most fearful the world has ever
seen, but the difference will be quantitative and not qual-
itative. God's people have always suffered persecution,
tribulation; why then should we expect God to change the
divine order which has marked the entire course of redemptive history? Why should God do something for the
Church at the end of the age when He has never done it before? Granted that the Great Tribulation and the sufferings which will be inflicted by the Antichrist will be more

fearful than anything previously experienced, yet they are not different in kind from all the tribulation and persecution of the ages. The final persecution of God's people by Antichrist is nothing but the consummation of the same hostility which the world and the prince of evil have manifested against God and His people throughout the entire course of the age. God will not deliver His people *from* such tribulation, but He will preserve them *in* it. Jesus assured His disciples of this fact. Even though they are put to death, not a hair of their head would perish (Lk. 21: 16-18). Physical death, bodily suffering is not to be feared, fearful as it is, by those who have been redeemed by the suffering and the death of Christ. Martyrdom has ever been a mark of faithfulness to Christ. Believers have been ready, often glad, to die for Christ's sake. Why should it be any different at the end?

8

RIGHTLY DIVIDING THE WORD

IN THIS brief chapter, we shall deal with the most important reason used by pretribulationists for refusing to apply the prophecies about the Great Tribulation to the Church. It is so important that it may be called the major premise of dispensationalism. It goes back to J. N. Darby, and is a method of handling the Scriptures which B. W. Newton, one of the earliest and most learned of the Brethren, called "the height of speculative nonsense." The most vigorous recent defense of pretribulationism devotes an early chapter to the establishment of this principle as the foundation for the entire subsequent discussion.

This principle has frequently been called, "Rightly dividing the Word of Truth." It is the method of deciding in advance which Scriptures deal with the Church and which Scriptures have to do with Israel, and then to interpret the passages concerned in the light of this "division" of the Word. "No one can possibly have a clear perception of Scripture as a whole, or of Bible prophecy in particular, who does not discern the distinction between two of the things that differ, namely, Israel and the Church."

In both Matthew and the Revelation where the Great Tribulation is prophesied, the people of God are seen in the Tribulation. They are to be put to flight by the Abomination of Desolation (Matt. 24:20). The Tribulation will bring martyrdom to the elect, a martyrdom so extensive that they would be wiped out except for the fact that God will shorten the days for their sake to spare them (Matt. 24:22). Spiritual deception will be so strong that it will lead astray, if possible, even the elect (Matt. 24:24). At the close of the Tribulation, when the Son of man comes in glory, He will send His angels to gather His elect from the four winds (Matt. 24:31).

In the midst of the Tribulation, God's elect will experience terrible suffering, and they will be finally delivered by the return of Christ. Who are the elect? Are they the Church, or Israel? Dispensationalism solves this problem by the application of its major premise. One of the most influential dispensationalist commentaries on Matthew begins the discussion of this chapter with these sentences: "The disciples knew absolutely nothing of a Christian age. Such an age could not even begin, when they asked the question about the end of the age. They did not mean a Christian age, but their Jewish age . . . . The reference to Daniel and the great tribulation, which never concerns the church, but Israel, shows us that we are not on Christian, but Jewish ground." Therefore, the references to the elect in Matthew 24 must be references to the elect of Israel, not to believers who are elected to salvation.

In the Revelation, the people of God are seen on earth suffering at the hands of Antichrist. The Beast is given power "to make war with the saints and to overcome them" (Rev. 13:7). The capital of the Beast is described as a woman "drunken with the blood of the martyrs of Jesus" (Rev. 17:6). Who are these saints who suffer martyrdom? Are they the Church or Israel?

Again, dispensationalists apply their major premise. "One difficulty so many postribulationists have is due to the fact that they get part of the book of Revelation in the grace age. . . . If we distinguish the ages and recognize the ground on which we stand, whether it be Jewish or Gentile, we will find little difficulty in relation to the issue in hand." Therefore we must conclude that the saints and martyrs are not the Church but Jews.

Back of this Jewish interpretation is the assumption that the Great Tribulation has to do exclusively with the Jews and not with the Church. It is the time of *Jacob's* trouble

(Jer. 30:7). It is the last week of the seventy in Daniel 9:25-27 which have to do with the destiny of Israel, not the Church. During the sixty-nine weeks, God was dealing with Israel; and in the last week, the seven years of the Great Tribulation, God will resume His dealings with Israel which, during the parenthesis of the church age, have been suspended. Since the seventieth week has to do with Israel, we must assume that the Church does not enter into the picture at all. The passages in Matthew 24 and the Revelation which predict the Tribulation have nothing to do with the Church; they are concerned altogether with Israel. Therefore, the words "elect" and "saints" are to be understood as belonging to Old Testament terminology, not to the New Testament age of grace and the Church.

To this line of reasoning, we must raise the question: Where does the Word of God *say* that the Great Tribulation is exclusively Jewish? Dispensationalists say this, but does the Word of God really assert this to be true? Is this an inference, or is it the express declaration of Scripture? There is very strong evidence which suggests that the Great Tribulation applies to the Church as well as to Israel.

The promise of the outpouring of the Holy Spirit was given by God through the prophet Joel to Israel. The prophecy looks forward to a national restoration of Judah and Jerusalem when God would pour out His Spirit upon all Israel, not only upon the few spiritual leaders of the nation. One would search in vain in Joel for any reference to the Church. The promise has to do with the final destiny of God's people, Israel. Yet dispensationalists usually recognize that this promise has a double fulfillment to the Church at Pentecost and to Israel at the end of the age. It "has a partial and continuous fulfillment during the 'last days' which began with the first advent of Christ; but the great fulfillment awaits the 'last days' as applied to Israel" (Scofield).

The same double fulfillment is to be recognized in the prophecy of the new covenant which God will write in the hearts of His people. As the prophecy was given in Jeremiah 31:31-34, it had to do only "with the house of Israel, and with the house of Judah." The Church does not appear in the prophecy at all. However, the Spirit of God Himself in Hebrews 8:7-13 applies this prophecy to the new covenant made by our Lord with the Church. Scofield recognizes that this prophecy, given exclusively to Israel, has its fulfillment in the Church, when he says of Hebrews 8:8, "The New Covenant rests upon the sacrifice of Christ, and secures the eternal blessedness, under the Abrahamic Covenant, of *all who believe*" (italics ours). The new covenant, promised in Jeremiah 31, was made by our Lord with the Church and is now in effect; and at the end of the age, Israel as a people will be saved and brought within the blessings of the new covenant.

If then we have the principle clearly established that prophecies which in the Old Testament have to do with God's future purpose for Israel have their fulfillment both in the Church and in Israel, why should we not conclude that the prophecies about the Great Tribulation which have to do in their prophetic form with Israel will find their fulfillment both in the Church and in Israel, unless the Word of God clearly asserts the contrary? We are on church ground, not Jewish ground in Acts 2 and Hebrews 8 even though the Old Testament predictions appear to be exclusively on Jewish ground. Why are we not also on church ground as well as on Jewish ground in Matthew 24 and Revelation 13? The assumption that this is exclusively Jewish ground is a human interpretation which is not supported by the Word of God.

This method of "dividing the Scriptures" leads to grave, and — we feel — insoluble difficulties. Not only is Matthew 24 thought to be Jewish, but so are the entire first twelve chapters, because they have to do with the "kingdom of the heavens" which Jesus offered to Israel; and this could be nothing but the earthly, millennial, Jewish kingdom. The Sermon of the Mount in Matthew 5-7 is not for the Church in the age of grace but for the Jew in the restored age of law in the Davidic kingdom.[1] If this is true, is Mark's Gospel also Jewish? And is Luke's Gospel Jewish too? Matthew was written for Jews, but Mark and Luke were written to Gentiles. Yet the "elect" are seen in the Great Tribulation in Mark 13:20, 27 even as in Matthew. Is this also Jewish ground? When Jesus said, as recorded in Luke 18:7, that God would avenge His elect, did He refer to Jews or to all the elect, all the company of the saved?

If Matthew, Mark, and Luke are on Jewish ground, then how much more John. The first three Gospels record Jesus' ministry in "Galilee of the gentiles," but John records the ministry in Jerusalem, the capital of Israel, the seat of the Temple of God. Is John's Gospel on Jewish ground too? If the first part of Matthew's Gospel recording the Galilean ministry is Jewish, then the first part of John's Gospel recording the Jerusalem ministry must also be Jewish, for it has to do with our Lord's ministry in the Holy City.

When Jesus told Jewish Nicodemus at the beginning of His ministry that he must be born again to see the kingdom of God, did He refer to the Davidic, millennial kingdom? Is this Jewish ground? Does the eternal life promised the believer (John 3:36) have reference to admission into the millennial, Davidic kingdom, as the same phrase in Matthew 25:46 is interpreted by dispensationalists to mean; or is it really eternal life — salvation in the age to come? Yet dispensationalism interprets John on church ground, not Jewish. Where does the Word of God say that Matthew is on Jewish ground but John on church ground? These are questions which anyone who is seeking a clear directive from Scripture instead of an inference asks without finding an answer.

---

1. The present author has dealt with this problem of the "postponed kingdom" at length in his book, *Crucial Questions About the Kingdom of God* (Grand Rapids: Eerdmans, 1952).

The same problem is raised in the book of Revelation. Where does the Word of God say that we have left behind the age of grace and have returned to Jewish ground? This inference is contradicted by the very key to the prophecy: the seven-sealed book. John saw a scroll, written on both sides, and sealed not with a single seal but with seven seals. We are not told what the book contained, but Walter Scott, foremost recent commentator on the Revelation of the dispensationalists, is right when he says that the books contain "the revelation of God's purpose and counsel concerning the world." What lies ahead for mankind? Where is the race headed for? Is it to go on forever like a book which has no final chapter? Is it to end in self-destruction like a book which breaks off in the middle of the plot? Or does the story have a real conclusion in which the problems are solved and the many threads of the narrative are picked up and woven together in a meaningful plot? The seven-sealed book of human destiny contains the answer.

Human history has a purpose, a destiny, a goal. The fact that the book is sealed suggested two things. Man does not write the story; that is, man cannot solve the problems of history. It must be God, not man, who authors the story of the consummation. Secondly, the future is a closed secret to man. He cannot of himself discover its contents. The future is a book both closed and tightly sealed. The goal of history, the future prophetic destiny of the race is God's story, not man's.

John wept much because no one was found who could open the book, who could read meaning and destiny in the prophetic future. Then One was found. He is the Lamb who has been slain. He is the Lion of Judah, the Root of David, i.e., the One foretold in Old Testament prophecy. He is the One who was slain and who purchased to God with His shed blood men of every tribe and tongue and people and nation (5:9-10). The Lamb of God who takes away the sin of the world holds the key to the future. Only because there was One who was willing to die upon the

cross is there One who can destroy Satan and sin and bring
the people of God into the blessedness of God's kingdom.
Were it not for the slain Lamb who is also the kingly
Lion, the world would be only the kingdom of evil. But
Christ will open the sealed book, bring judgment upon the
prince and the kingdom of evil, and bring the redeemed
into the kingdom of God. This is history's divinely decreed
destiny.

The book of Revelation places the grace of God, dis-
played in the slain Lamb and the redemption freely provided, squarely in the center of the future. The Lamb of
God alone can solve the enigma of human history. He a-
lone can bring God's purposes to their consummation. This
is the central theme of the Revelation. This destiny does
indeed concern Israel, and "all Israel" is destined to be
saved. It also concerns "men of every tribe, and tongue,
and people, and nation" (5:9). It concerns all men. No
reason appears in the Revelation to interpret this prophecy
on Jewish ground; but the centrality of the Lamb of God
who redeems by His blood men from *every nation* suggests
that we are on church ground, the age of salvation and
grace.

Scripture says nothing about the end of the church age
and a restoration of the Jewish age. Therefore the conclusion that the saints seen in the Tribulation are not the
New Testament saints of Revelation 19:8 but are Old
Testament saints in the person of restored Israel is an inference, not the assertion of the Word of God; and it is an
inference which appears to contradict the indications of
Scripture.

There appears to be no valid reason, therefore,—no
assertion of Scripture which would require or even suggest
that we must apply the prophecies about the Tribulation
to a restored Jewish nation rather than to the redeemed of
the New Testament, the Church. On the contrary, we have
ample reason to apply the prophecies about the Great Tribulation both to Israel and to the Church.

9

THE BLESSED HOPE

THE REASON why pretribulationism has held such an important place in prophetic teaching is that it has been thought to be inseparable from premillennialism and from the Biblical doctrine of the Lord's personal, visible return. Christians have felt that the only alternative to a pretribulation position was a liberal doctrine which discounts the hope of Christ's second coming.

While it is true that the modern emphasis on the Lord's return has been strongly supported by men who held to a pretribulation rapture, this fact does not prove that the teaching is Biblical or essential to premillennial doctrine.

The one question ultimately must be, What does the Word of God actually teach? and not, What have men taught? The teaching which is absolutely essential, because it is Biblical, is that of the personal, visible, glorious return of Christ to bring the kingdom of God. If one holds to this hope, he has lost nothing essential to Christian life and doctrine even though he does not hold to a pretribulation rapture. On the contrary, the teaching of pretribulationism and the undue emphasis which is being placed on some of these details of eschatology are attended by certain grave dangers.

First, the contemporary concern with the question of the Rapture and the Tribulation has overshadowed the really important questions having to do with the Blessed Hope itself. The preoccupation of students of the Bible with such details incurs the risk of losing sight of far more important issues. It is a tragedy of the first order that those who "love his appearing" are dissipating their energies contending about such questions when the doctrine of Christ's coming itself is today under heavy attack.

One of the most highly lauded and honored missionaries in the world today is Albert Schweitzer. Let it be admitted that we should give due recognition to the man's eminence of character, to the spirit of self-sacrificial humanitarianism he has manifested in turning his back upon a fabulously successful career in Europe to bury himself in the African jungles to minister to the bodies of men in their sicknesses and sufferings. Nevertheless, it must also be pointed out that this same famous man has written a book which has proven to be one of the most influential volumes of our generation in which Jesus is portrayed as a deluded fanatic, a man who tragically sacrificed himself to fantastic apocalyptic conceptions that the world was at once to come to an end, when he would be raised to heaven to be a heavenly messianic son of man. To Schweitzer, the Jesus who actually lived in history is an offense, not a savior. In many circles today, young men are being taught this is the actual Jesus who lived on earth. For Christianity deriving from such a deluded personage, any teaching of a second coming of Christ is at once fantastic and impossible.

A very different interpretation is prevalent in Great Britain today. Students are taught that everything men used to look for at the return of the Lord in His messianic kingdom has now become available to men in and through the Church. "All that the church hoped for in the second coming of Christ is already given in its present experience of Christ through the Spirit." The author recently asked a minister from the Church of England with whom he shared a Bible conference how influential this view was in Great Britain, and he replied that it was the only view which many students were taught. This view means "that it is impossible ever to revive the belief that the Lord would in literal truth arrive to judgment upon the clouds of heaven during the thirties of the first century. He did not do so. To work up a fantastic expectation that He will arrive in the thirties of the twentieth century is not primitive Christianity, whatever it may be."

The impact of liberalism upon American Christian thought may be seen in this statement by one of the most learned men in an outstanding theological seminary: "He (Jesus) was certainly no mad fanatic, no deluded pretender to a celestial and really mythical title, no claimant to a throne which did not exist, no prophet of a coming judgment to be carried out by a heavenly figure seated on the clouds with whom he identified himself—which judgment never took place, never could take place."

While assaults like these are being directed against the fundamental doctrine of the personal return of the Lord, it is almost a fantastic thing that men who love His appearing and recognize its indispensable place in Christian doctrine are off in a corner disputing among themselves about the details which will attend Christ's return, when they ought to be standing shoulder to shoulder in defense of the doctrine of the second coming of Christ itself. How helpful it would be if we could see a great prophetic Bible conference whose purpose was designed to make an impact upon the Christian Church at large in behalf of the essential place of the doctrine of the second coming of Christ in Christian life and thought. What a contribution to the study of the Word and to real Christian unity if instead of dedicating itself to the objective of propagating a pretribulation type of eschatology, the prophetic conference movement was really concerned to hear both sides of the question and to place its emphasis on the great fundamental essentials held by all who believe the Word and hold the Blessed Hope.

Many Christians believe, and without doubt sincerely, that any deviation from the popular pretribulation teaching is a step away from the Word of God toward liberalism. This belief does not square with the facts. It is said that liberals are never found among premillennialists but are often found among a- and postmillennialists. This, however, is not an accurate representation of the situation. A man who is a theological liberal will not call himself an amillennialist any more than he will a premillennialist. An amillennialist is one who shares with the premillennialist the real hope of the visible, personal, glorious return of Christ to inaugurate the final stages of the kingdom of God. Amillennialism and premillennialism stand together in the insistence that salvation will never be brought to its consummation and the kingdom of God come in its fullness without the personal, visible return of the same Jesus who was taken up into heaven. *No theological liberal will share this* doctrine. "There is a considerable morbid interest attaching to many of the discussions about the future. Christians may learn better how to employ their time if they will look about them at the world's present dire need. The future may well enough be left to take care of itself." Thus writes one of the more "conservative" liberals of the present day. To such a man, the entire discussion over pre- and amillennialism is an occupation for fanatics, not for modern scholars.

Any man who will accept the designation "amillennialist" is not a liberal, for he is looking for the personal glorious second coming of Christ. The entire debate over the question of whether or not there will be a literal millennium or an earthly kingdom after the return of Christ has nothing to do with the distinction between an orthodox and a liberal theology. Only men who believe in a prophetic Scripture, inspired by the Holy Spirit, will debate the question. Was B. B. Warfield moving toward liberalism because he was a postmillennialist? Was J. Gresham Machen any less a fundamentalist because he was an amillennialist? We must not lose our perspective nor permit our attention to be diverted from the main issues of the day to those which are relatively unimportant.

The man who believes that the kingdom of God is to be fully realized only by the visible personal return of the Lord will not preach a social gospel of liberalism whose object is to build the kingdom of God. Perhaps postmillennialism is in danger of moving in that direction. There may be close similarities between the idea of christianizing the world by the preaching of the Gospel (postmillennialism) and that of christianizing the world by building the kingdom of God (the social gospel), although there need not be. Postmillennialism, for all its apparent similarity to the social gospel, can be thoroughly supernaturalistic in its understanding of Christ and the Gospel. This was certainly true of Warfield.

However, both the amillennialist and the premillennalist insist that the world is evil, that the business of the Church primarily is to preach the Gospel of salvation, and that the Christian must be living in constant expectation of the personal second coming of Christ. The fullness of the kingdom will come only with the coming of the King. This is Biblical doctrine, and on it premillennialists, whether they believe in a pre- or posttribulation rapture, and amillennialists stand together.

Secondly, a teaching of a pretribulation rapture is not essential for the preservation of the purifying influence of the Blessed Hope. Many of God's people are sincerely afraid that unless they hold to a pretribulation, any-moment coming of Christ, this doctrine will no longer be a purifying hope. They fear that an event which cannot take place until the end of the Tribulation and which therefore cannot occur at any moment cannot exercise the purifying influence upon the lives of believers which the Scriptures teach.

We must again ask, What does the Bible really teach? Is it the fact of the coming of Christ or its imminence which is a purifying hope? The Word of God does not teach that it is the any-moment character of the coming of Christ which is to exercise a purifying influence; it is the glorious reality of that coming itself.

The one verse which explicitly sets forth this purifying hope is I John 3:2, 3: "We know that if he shall be manifested, we shall be like him; for we shall see him even as he is. And everyone that hath this hope set on him puri- fieth himself, even as he is pure." The incentive of this verse is not the fear of being caught in some sort of im- purity at the moment when Christ comes. It is rather the hope of being like Christ whenever He comes which exer- cises the purifying influence. Because I have my hope set on Christ, because I know that I shall be like Him, be- cause He is the object of my affection, I purify myself even as He is pure.

It is to be emphasized, furthermore, that if we take this verse at its face value, the time we shall see our Lord as He is, is at His "manifestation." "If he shall be manifested, we shall be like him; for we shall see him even as he is." This word "to make manifest" is used frequently of the appear- ance of our Lord in the flesh (I Tim. 3:16, II Tim. 1:10, Heb. 9:26, I Pet. 1:20). Certainly this was a manifes- tation of the Son of God for all to see. It was not limited to believers. The verb is used of the second coming of Christ outside of I John only in Colossians 3:4: "When Christ, who is our life, shall be manifested, then shall ye also with him be mainfested in glory." Of this verse, Dr. Ironside says, "He is coming back to the earth that rejected Him, and all His saints are coming with Him, not, of course, to take up human conditions here in the world again; but in resurrection bodies to appear with Him before the aston- ished eyes of those who still reject Him." This manifesta- tion, says Dr. Ironside, is described in I Thessalonians 1:5-11. With this we agree. We are therefore led to the in- escapable conclusion that our purifying hope is that of be- coming like Christ when we shall see Him at His manifes- tation or Revelation at the end of the Tribulation period. The Blessed Hope is therefore not the Rapture of the Church, unless the Rapture and Revelation are identical in time.

A recent article defending pretribulationism says, "If any part of it (the Tribulation) must be fulfilled before the

Rapture, then the Scriptures which speak of our expectancy of seeing Him imminently are nullified and the exhortations to godly living, based on this expectancy, lose their power. For the hope of our Lord's imminent coming carries with it a restraint upon the flesh and an incentive to a Spirit-filled walk that are not found in any other doctrine of the Scriptures." This author then quotes Titus 2:12-14 to prove his point, "Instructing us, to the intent that, denying ungodliness and worldly lusts, we should live soberly and righteously and godly in this present world; looking for the blessed hope and appearing of the glory of . . . Jesus Christ."

To this, three things are to be said. Firstly, this passage does not use the second coming of Christ as the main incentive for godly living. The main incentive is the fact that "the grace of God hath appeared, bringing salvation to all men" (vs. 11). In this Scripture, our purity results not from the return of Christ, but because Christ "gave himself for us, that he might redeem us from all iniquity, and purify unto himself a people for his own possession, zealous of good works" (vs. 14). The present author has no intention of suggesting that the coming of Christ is not a purifying hope, but he must insist that this is not the main teaching of this passage. We are to be pure *because we have been redeemed*, purchased unto God by the shed blood of Jesus Christ. We are to be pure because we no longer belong to the world, or to sin, or to ourselves; we belong to God. We are His own special possession. Because we belong to God, we are living in expectancy of the appearing of our great God and Savior, Jesus Christ. We long to see Him who has redeemed us. We no longer belong to the world, but as citizens of heaven, we desire eagerly to enter into the full experience of what heavenly citizenship means. Citizenship in the world means weak, corruptible bodies; but the perfection of heavenly citizenship means the transformation of the body when humiliation is exchanged for glory. Thus we long for the return of Christ.

Secondly, the coming of Christ which is referred to in Titus 2:13 is not the alleged secret any-moment coming; it is rather the epiphany of His glory which pretribulationists admit occurs at the end of the Tribulation. Yet the Word of God explicitly says that we are to *look for* an event which is to be preceded by the Tribulation.

Thirdly, the idea of the restraining influence of the imminent, "any-moment" coming of Christ, as frequently interpreted, suggests that the highest motive for Christian conduct and for separation from the world is that of fear. Since the Lord may come at any moment, I do not dare to do some things I would like to do and might otherwise do, lest He come and catch me.

Undoubtedly, the motive of fear has its place in Christian experience, and our Lord Himself warned men to fear Him who is able to cast both body and soul into hell (Matt. 10:28). An element of warning is indeed found in the commands to watch in Matthew 24:36ff; but the warning is not grounded upon the fact that the return of Christ may occur at any moment, for the coming of the Son of man (vs. 44) is His coming on the clouds with power and great glory at the end of the Tribulation. Furthermore, the warning is not directed to disciples who are becoming careless; it is *addressed to those who are not really disciples at all.*

In the days of Noah, the signs of approaching judgment were evident. The ark was arising before the eyes of wicked men; and Noah's preaching of imminent judgment was the clearest sign of all. Yet the day came upon men when they "knew not . . . and took them all away; so shall be the coming of the Son of man. Then shall two men be in the field; one is taken, and one is left; two women shall be grinding at the mill; one is taken, and one is left. Watch therefore; for ye know not on what day your Lord cometh" (vv. 39, 42). Whether this refers to being taken by rapture or by judgment, the separation involved is between true and false disciples, between believers and unbelievers, not between consecrated and worldly Christians. The mo-

tive of fear is not addressed to the disciple of the Lord, but
to the unbeliever. The motive inspiring the believer to a
holy walk is not the fear of being apprehended by a sudden
return of the Lord in some worldly conduct, but the joy of
meeting the Lord who has redeemed us. It is our love for
Him and the joy of the anticipated consummation of perfect fellowship which impels us to a pure life. This is the
thought of Titus 2:11-14.

The motive of shame is indeed employed in I John 2:28.
"And now, my little children, abide in him; that, if he
shall be manifested, we may have boldness, and not be
ashamed before him at his coming." But it is the shame
which can only hurt love. And the possibility of being
shamed in the presence of Christ is not related to an imminent, any-moment coming but rather to His person whenever He is manifested.

It is often maintained that an event cannot exercise a
direct influence upon my life unless it is able to take place
at any moment. As plausible as this reasoning sounds, it
does not square with the Scripture or with experience.
Peter directs the attention of his readers to the day of God
when "the heavens being on fire shall be dissolved and the
elements shall melt with fervent heat." This day of God
will bring the final consummation of God's purposes at the
end of the millennium, and speaking of this day, Peter
says, "We look for a new heavens and a new earth, wherein dwelleth righteousness." This objective is at least a
thousand years away. Yet Peter says, "seeing that these
things are thus all to be dissolved, what manner of persons
ought ye to be in *all holy living and godliness,* looking for
and earnestly desiring the coming of the day of God" (II
Peter 3:11-13). It is the character and the certainty of the
final consummation when there will at last be a new earth
which has no room for unrighteousness which is the mo-
tivation for holy living and godliness; for it is only the holy,
godly man who can expect to have a place in this new earth
wherein dwelleth righteousness.

Perhaps the author may be permitted to illustrate the
continuing influence of a future event from his personal experience. When he was a freshman in college, he fell in
love with a girl who three and a half years later became his
wife. He knew the wedding day was more than three years
away. There were intervals when they could not be together for months at a time and there were indeed lonely
hours; but they both knew that the day would come when
they would be together as man and wife and when their love
would find its full realization in the formation of a home.
If any one suggests that this affection, even though it would
not be brought to its normal fruition for more than three
years, did not exercise a continual and deep influence upon
my life, he does not know what love is. During those years
I had no serious interest in any other. I had given my love
to one, there was no room for another.

The hope of the Christian is "the Marriage of the Lamb"
when faith shall be translated into sight, when our love
for Christ shall be brought to its consummation in that
happy day. However, it is not primarily the day itself which
exercises the purifying hope so much as it is the Person
with whom we shall be united; and we have already given
our affection and love to Him. The verse in I John 3:3 does
not say, "and everyone that hath this hope *within himself*
purifieth himself," as the King James translation might
suggest. It reads, "and everyone that hath this hope *set
on Christ* purifieth himself, even as Christ is pure." It is
the Lord who is the object of our hope; and whether His
coming be near or far, the glorious fact of His person and
the certainty of our union with Him is the ground and the
incentive for our holy walk.

Third, pretribulationism sacrifices one of the main mo-
tives for world-wide missions, viz., hastening the attainment of the Blessed Hope. The pretribulation doctrine as
it is usually taught robs the Church of one of the most dy-
namic incentives for world-wide evangelization. At the Sec-

ond New York Congress on Prophecy held in 1943, Samuel
M. Zwemer gave an address on the subject "The Return of
our Lord and World-wide Evangelism." His text was Matthew 24:14, "And this gospel of the kingdom shall be
preached in the whole world for a testimony unto all nations
and then shall the end come." It is doubtful whether Zwemer
would be invited to give this address in a modern prophetic
conference, for according to the usual pretribulation interpretation, Matthew 24:14 does not belong to the Church but
to the Jewish remnant which will be brought into existence
after the Rapture of the Church to be the witness for God
to the nations after the Church has been taken away. The
"Gospel of the Kingdom" is said to be not the Gospel of
grace by which we are saved, but the good news that the
millennial kingdom is about to be established. Within a
period of seven years, the Jewish remnant, although lacking the indwelling power of the Holy Spirit — for according to the theory, the Spirit has been taken out of the world
at the Rapture of the Church — will evangelize the entire
world with this announcement about the coming kingdom.
This task the Christian Church, *indwelt by the Spirit of
God, has failed* thus far to accomplish in two thousand
years.

This interpretation which applies Matthew 24:14 to a
Jewish remnant is an inference and not the clear teaching
of the Word of God. It has not been proven that the Gospel
of the Kingdom is anything other than redeeming grace.
Almost the same phrase is found in Acts 8:12 where we
read that Philip went to Samaria, "gospeling concerning
the kingdom of God and the name of Jesus Christ." The
one great mission of the Church is to evangelize the world.
This is not a theory, it is a fact. Jesus gave the Church its
marching orders to go and make disciples of all nations;
and in carrying out the task, He promised to be with them
even unto the end of the age (Matt. 28:19, 20).

Matthew 24:14 conveys the same thought. The good news about the kingdom of God [1] must be carried into the whole world for a witness to all nations. This is the divinely appointed task of the Church. The Church is not to save the world; it is not to christianize the world; it is not to transform the world so that it becomes the kingdom of God. This will be accomplished only by the glorious second coming of Christ. Until Christ comes, this age remains an evil age (Gal. 1:4) under the influence of Satan (II Cor. 4:4). The Church's task must ever be carried out in frank recognition of the character of the age. Nevertheless it has a task which is divinely given and in which the Church must be victorious: world-wide evangelization and the gathering of the saved into the body of Christ. Only when this commission has been completed will Christ return. Those who "love His appearing" are those who should have the greatest concern for the evangelization of the world.

Christ is tarrying until the Church has completed its task. When Matthew 24:14 has been fulfilled, then Christ will come. There is no more notable "sign of the times" than the fact that the greatest impetus in world-wide evangelization since apostolic times has taken place in the preceding century. The world is nearly evangelized; *any generation which is really dedicated to the task can complete the mission.* The Lord can come in our own generation, in our life-time — if we stir ourselves and finish our task. Let us then not be dissipating our energies in differences over the Rapture and the Tribulation. Rather let every believer who cherishes the Blessed Hope give himself in unstinted measure to the prosecution of world-evangelization; for then will Christ come.

How can anyone say that posttribulationism cuts the nerve of foreign missions? How can anyone accuse posttribulationism of lacking evangelistic drive? The opposite is the case. It is impossible to conceive of a stronger mo-

---

1. See John 3:3; Acts 20:25; 28:23, 31; Rom. 14:17; I Cor. 4:20; Col. 1:13; Heb. 12:28.

tive for world evangelization and for the salvation of the lost than the realization that Christ is waiting to return until the Church has completed this mission.

The author is not alone in this conviction. Listen to the roll-call of some of the mightiest missionary statesmen and men of God of our generation. R. H. Glover, Home Director of the China Inland Mission said, "Christ did not return at the end of the first generation, nor has He yet returned after 1900 years, the obvious reason being that there were still millions then, and there are still millions today, who have never heard the Gospel."

G. W. Playfair, General Director of the Sudan Interior Mission, said, "Does the Lord delay His Coming? Yes, and for only one reason. Until an unfaithful Church awakes fully to the fact that the Gospel 'must first be published among all nations,' until His Church is complete, and it cannot be complete from the favored half of the world which has heard the Gospel. The Church will only be complete by receiving into its membership men of every nation, language and people."

Charles R. Erdman, of Princeton Theological Seminary, said, "In spite of all differences and disturbances, the work of his followers is to be pressed. Their task is clear. Until it has been completed, the King will not return. Whatever differences of opinion may exist among the servants of the King relative to the details of his return, all should be united in the accomplishment of their common task and inspired by the same blessed hope."

Samuel H. Kellogg, in his strong defense of premillennialism against postmillennialism entitled, *Are Premillennialists Right?*, wrote, "The Premillennialist believes, no less than those who differ with him, that the Gospel must be published among all nations before the kingdom will come. Premillennialism furnishes (a motive for world wide evangelization) of great power peculiar to that doctrine. It makes the appearance of the glorious kingdom a practical possibility of the near future, as the contrary doctrine cannot. For to convert the world in our own time is not in man; but to witness to all nations is in the power of the Church, even in this generation. We believe that, if but that be done, the Lord will come, and with Him the great victory of the ages, the first resurrection and the everlasting kingdom. We believe this, because we find it plainly declared by our Lord Himself, that when 'this Gospel of the kingdom shall be preached for a witness to all nations, then shall the end come.' "

One of the most zealous and successful promoters of the modern missionary movement is Oswald J. Smith. Billy Graham says of Dr. Smith, "As a missionary statesman he has no peer. Around the world the name Oswald J. Smith symbolizes world-wide evangelization . . . . As a missionary he exemplifies a passion for souls." This judgment few will question.

In his recent book, *The Passion for Souls,* Dr. Smith has a chapter entitled, "Will Christ Return to Earth Before the World has been Evangelized?" in which he takes as his texts Mark 13:10 and Matthew 24:14. He refuses to recognize the dispensational difference between the Gospel of grace and the Gospel of the Kingdom. He says, "I am preaching both the Gospel of the grace of God *and* the Gospel of the Kingdom, constantly. The Gospel of the grace of God is the good news that Jesus died for sinners. The Gospel of the Kingdom is the good news that Jesus is coming back to reign. Both messages must be proclaimed; and whether it is the Gospel of the grace of God or the Gospel of the Kingdom, it makes no difference. In both cases, it is the Gospel, the good news. And it must be published before the end comes."

Under the heading "A Dangerous Heresy," Dr. Smith says, "But I know what some are saying. I hear it everywhere. They are saying: 'This is not the task of the Church at all, the Jews are to do it; we should leave it for them after we have been raptured away.'

"I know of no heresy that can do more to cut the nerve of missionary endeavour. Moreover, I know of no definite statement in the entire Bible that would lead me to believe for one single moment, that the Jews are to evangelize the world during the days of the great tribulation, as some people seem to think. Were I to believe that I would fold my arms and do nothing.

"Do you mean to say that after the Holy Spirit has gone, and we are told that He is to go when the Church goes, do you mean to say that the Jews can accomplish more in some seven years or less, without the help of the Holy Spirit, in the midst of persecution and martyrdom, than we have been able to accomplish in nearly two thousand years, with the Holy Spirit's aid, when it has been easy to be a Christian? Preposterous! Impossible!

. . . .

"Christ wants to return. He longs to reign. It is His right. Then why does He wait? He is waiting for you and me to complete the task. He is waiting for us to do what He has told us to do. Many a time He must say to Himself as He sits there, 'How long, I wonder, are they going to keep Me waiting? When will they let Me come back? How soon can I return to earth to sit on My throne and reign?'

. . . .

"This then is His answer to their question. 'What shall be THE sign of thy coming, and the end of the age?' That was what they wanted to know — THE sign preceding and indicating the end. His answer to their question in verse 3 of Matthew xxiv is found in verse 14. Here it is: 'This gospel shall be preached *in all the world,* for a witness unto *all nations;* and THEN shall the end come.' All His other predictions indicate the *approaching* end; this one, THE end . . . . It is God's programme: first world evangelization; then, the reign of Christ."

A. B. Simpson is one of the great saints of modern times. He wrote, "The work of missions is the great means of hastening that end (the return of Christ). The work of the Holy Ghost through the church was chiefly intended to gather out from all nations a people for His name, a bride for the Lamb. . . . Until the whole number of His elect shall have thus been called and gathered home, He cannot come. . . . . We know that our missionary work is not in vain, but, in addition to the blessing it is to bring to the souls we lead to Christ, best of all it is to bring Christ Himself back again. It puts in our hands the key to the bridal chamber and the lever that will hasten His return. What a glorious privilege. What a mighty incentive. Do we long to see Him in His glory and to meet our loved ones once more? Then we shall work with redoubled energy to spread the Gospel, to tell the story, to evangelize the world and to 'prepare the way of the Lord.' "

> O Let us then His coming haste!
> O let us end this awful waste
>   Of souls that never die!
> A thousand millions still are lost,
> A Saviour's blood has paid the cost.
>   O hear their dying cry!
>
> The Master's coming draweth near,
> The Son of man will soon appear,
>   His Kingdom is at hand.
> But ere that glorious day can be,
> This Gospel of the Kingdom we
>   Must preach in every land.
>   (A. B. Simpson).

Fourth, an attitude of expectancy is not identical with a belief in an any-moment coming of Christ. There will doubtless be some who read this book who will say that its position discourages an attitude of expectancy because it does not support the view of an any-moment coming.

This attitude is based on a false assumption: that belief in the any-moment return of Christ is identical with a Biblical attitude of expectancy.

We would meet this possible criticism by an *ad hominem* argument. The fact is that those who teach the usual pattern of a pretribulation rapture cannot consistently hold to a true any-moment coming of Christ. According to their view, the final seven years before the millennium are the seventieth week of Daniel 9. Since these seventy weeks have to do exclusively with the destinies of Israel, the seventieth week has nothing to do with the Christian Church or the age of grace. One of the most consistent presentations of this position is that of C. L. Fowler in his *Building the Dispensations* (1940) where the period of tribulation is made a separate dispensation intervening between that of the "Body" (the church age) and the "Kingdom." Since the "Tribulation Age" has to do with Israel alone, we must conclude that the Church is to be raptured at its beginning. Thus no prophetic events are to take place before the secret coming of Christ to rapture the Church. All of the predicted events attending Christ's return will take place during the seven years following the Rapture. The next prophetic event, therefore, after the Ascension of Christ is the Rapture. No signs will herald its approach. It is a "signless" event. Therefore it could occur at any moment after the Ascension.

So the argument runs. But it overlooks one very important fact. According to this system, the Rapture occurs at the beginning of the seventieth week predicted in Daniel 9:27: "And he (Antichrist) shall make a firm covenant with many (the Jews) for one week; and in the midst of the week he shall cause the sacrifice and the oblation to cease." The last seven years begins when Antichrist — who is not yet recognized as such — makes a covenant with Israel, now restored in Palestine as a nation. In the "midst of the week," i.e., after three and a half years, Antichrist manifests himself as such, breaks the covenant, compels the Jews to discontinue their sacrifices, and launches the terrible persecution of the Great Tribulation.

If this is a correct interpretation of the prophetic future, *the Rapture of the Church is not the next event upon the prophetic calendar;* it is rather the return of Israel to her land. The Rapture of the Church is then preceded by a sign, the "sign of the fig tree," the sign of Israel. After the fall of Jerusalem in 70 A.D. and the destruction of the Jewish state and after the dissolution of the Roman empire, the Rapture could not take place until Israel was restored to Palestine as a nation and until there arose another emperor or king who would rule over all Europe. In other words, it would have been impossible for Christ to have returned to rapture the Church during the nineteenth century, or even as late as 1900 when the Turk was ruling Palestine and the Jew was scattered over the earth outside the land. It is furthermore quite impossible to imagine the machinery being set in motion to dislodge the Turk, to reverse the course of history and open Palestine to the Jew, to reassemble a few hundred thousand Jews in the land, to forge a national entity out of the heterogeneous people, to see an Antichrist arise out of the relatively stable European political scene who would dominate the continent and enter into covenant with restored Israel — all within a few months; and precisely this would be demanded by a true any-moment theory which would admit that Christ could have returned in 1900. Such a complex of historical events is conceivable in a generation, but hardly in a few months.

A real "any-moment" expectation is neither Biblically nor historically sound. This is not to say that we are not to be possessed with a spirit of expectancy. The Word is full of such an attitude. No man can possess a Biblical outlook without looking for the personal coming of the Lord. Paul taught the Thessalonians to "wait for his Son from heaven" (I Thess. 1:10). The word used is instructive. It is a word which would not be used of a patient sitting in a dentist's office waiting his turn to sit in the dentist's chair; nor of a sick man dying of an incurable disease, resignedly waiting the end. The word involves eagerness, longing, expectancy. It expresses an earnestness and intensity of desire which is to be the attitude of every believer toward the Blessed Hope.

That this attitude is not based on an any-moment expectation is shown by the objects of hope. We are looking eagerly not only for events which will occur, according to pretribulationism, at the Rapture (Rom. 8:23; Gal. 5:5; Phil. 3:20; Heb. 9:28); we are also looking eagerly for the Revelation of Christ at the end of the Tribulation (I Cor. 1:7). We are also looking for the day of God, the new heavens and the new earth which will come only after the millennium (II Pet. 3:12-13. A different but similar word is here used.)

There is in fact in the Word of God a tension, a "dialectic," a balance of two attitudes. This may be best illustrated by our Lord's teachings. He admonished to watchfulness because of the uncertainty of the day and hour of the coming of the Son of man. Yet he also taught explicitly that a long time would intervene between His departure and His return. When He came to Jerusalem for the last time, the people thought the kingdom of God was immediately to appear; but to correct their false "any-moment" expectation, He uttered a parable of a "certain nobleman [who] went into a *far* country, to receive for himself a kingdom, and to return" (Luke 19:12). Again, He illustrated His departure from earth and His second coming by a parable of a man going into another country, who entrusted to his servants his goods; and "*after a long time* the lord of those servants cometh, and maketh a reckoning with them" (Matt. 25:19). Furthermore, such sayings as Mark 13:10 and Matthew 24:14 about the proclamation of the Gospel in all the world, and Luke 21:24 about the times of the Gentiles involve a considerable historical perspective.

There is in our Lord's teachings a twofold emphasis: expectancy and perspective. He wished to leave every generation of His people in the position where they might feel that their generation might be the last and yet be unable to set dates. The reaction which this should create is seen in the Apostle Paul. Paul lived his entire life with an attitude of expectancy toward the return of Christ. He talks as though his generation would witness the end; yet he nowhere expressly affirms that the end will come in his lifetime. On the other hand, he has a long-range historical perspective. He sees the salvation of the Gentiles and then the final salvation of Israel. Paul lived as though Christ were coming back in his own generation; but he worked and planned as though the world would go on for a long time.

This is the Biblical tension; and this is the attitude God would find in every generation. The author has the conviction that we are now living in the last days. The restoration of Israel, the progress of world-wide evangelization, the contemporary deification of the state, the inroads of rationalistic thought in the Christian Church which may be an element in the apostasy — all these appear to be preparing the stage for the end in a way which no previous generation has witnessed. The Lord may well return within our lifetime. But we do not *know* that this is to be the case. If we knew we had only a few years, we would do some things differently. Life insurance and savings for retirement would be of no need if the Lord *is* to return within a few years. The investment of large amounts of money in the erection of church buildings, the creation of an indigenous church on the mission field, or the building of a theological seminary with its necessary buildings, library, etc., are unwise if the Lord is to appear within a decade. All of these are long-range projects. If we *know* that the world has only a few more years, nothing else counts. The Thessalonians were right.

Work, savings and planning for the future are all beside the point; there is no future to plan for.

The Biblical attitude is expressed by Paul in his first letter to the Thessalonians. It is a working faith, a laboring love, *and* a patient hope. While we "wait for his Son from heaven," the Word is to sound forth into all the world (I Thess. 1:3, 9-10). Expectancy — perspective; this pleases God, avoids error, and motivates to Christian service.

Fifth, pretribulationism misinterprets the Blessed Hope. The second coming of Christ and the expectation of entering into a perfected fellowship with Him when we shall see Him face to face is the Blessed Hope of the Church. Perhaps the most common objection raised against a posttribulation teaching is this. The second coming of Christ is no longer a Blessed Hope if the Church must first pass through the Tribulation. If we must look for tribulation rather than for a rapture before the Tribulation, then the Blessed Hope has lost its blessed character and becomes instead a day of dread and fear.

In answer to this position, two things are to be said. First, we have already demonstrated that the Church will not experience the wrath of God. The Great Tribulation so far as it involves the outpouring of God's wrath will not engulf the Church. If that were not the case, the Tribulation would be an experience of unimaginable horror. However, God has not destined us to wrath but to obtain salvation through our Lord Jesus Christ.

Secondly, the Word of God *does not teach that the Blessed Hope of the Church is a hope of deliverance from persecution.* The coming of Christ is described as the Blessed Hope in one verse: Titus 2:13. "Looking for the blessed hope and appearing of the glory of our great God and Saviour Jesus Christ." Did the Spirit of God know what He was doing when He inspired these words? Did He give to Paul a vague thought leaving him to confuse it with inaccurate language? We think not. The Blessed

Hope is not deliverance from tribulation; it is not even the Rapture itself; it is the epiphany, the outshining of the glory of our great God and Savior. If this verse is any guide, the Blessed Hope is not a secret coming of Christ; it is not the resurrection of the dead; it is not the transformation of the living; it is not the catching up of the Church; the Blessed Hope is the glorious epiphany of *Our Lord Himself*, which occurs at the end of the Great Tribulation.

To insist that the Blessed Hope must be escape from the Great Tribulation is to place the emphasis where the Scripture does not place it; it is in fact to impose an interpretation upon the Scripture in place of what the Word of God actually says. As we indicated in an earlier chapter, the Word of God everywhere assures us that in this age we are to expect tribulation and persecution. The last great persecution of Antichrist will indeed be worse and more fearful than anything the world has ever seen; but when we contemplate the history of martyrdom, why should we ask deliverance from what millions have already suffered? When we read in the books of the Maccabees of the tortures inflicted upon the Jews who were faithful to the teachings of the Law by the manifestation of antichrist in the Syrian king Antiochus Epiphanes; when we recall the thousands of Christians who fell in torture and death and did it gladly in the name of Christ at the hands of the manifestation of the spirit of antichrist in the Roman emperors; when we are reminded of the Inquisition with its rack and wheel and flame; when we remember from our own generation the liquidation of several millions of Jews by a modern antichrist, and even more recently the martyrdom of tens of thousands of Korean Christians, what kind of a faith does the Church of today exemplify and what sort of a gospel is it which we proclaim if we insist that God must deliver us from the hands of the last manifestation of antichrist at the end of the age?

There is one very sobering question which weighs heavily upon the writer's heart, and he would ask his readers to share it. Many of God's people are being assured today that the Rapture will take place before the Tribulation and that the Church will not experience those terrible days. Those who hold a different view and believe that the Church will suffer in the Tribulation from Antichrist have not been vocal. The author knows of a good number of outstanding Christian leaders who hold this expectation, but they do not wish to be quoted and they have not publicly expressed themselves.

However, can we afford to be silent on this question? In light of the fact that the Word of God nowhere expressly asserts a pretribulation rapture, and since there is no plain affirmation that the Church will be taken out of the world before Antichrist appears, let us suppose that we are in fact in the very last days, and within a matter of months or a few years at most, God moves upon the events of world history so that suddenly a new Caesar or Mussolini or Hitler or Stalin appears who is unquestionably the Antichrist. Suppose that such a person, the incarnation of satanic power, actually gains domination of the entire world as neither Mussolini or Hitler or Stalin were able to do. Suppose that he uses this power to demand a worship of himself and his state upon penalty of death. Suppose that martyrs begin to fall by the hundreds of thousands, not only of Jews but particularly of Christians who will not worship the Beast or receive his mark. Suppose that suddenly the people of God find themselves engulfed in a horrible persecution at the hands of the Antichrist when they had been assured repeatedly on the authority of the Word of God that this experience would never befall them. What will be the result? We leave it to the reader's imagination. Certainly we dare not propagate a teaching of safety about which the Word of God is not indisputably clear, nor should we accept the responsibility of filling the hearts of God's people with what may be a false hope and thus leave them utterly unprepared for terrible days of persecution when and if they fall. If there is the possibility that the Church is to suffer tribulation at the hands of Antichrist, do not those who believe it have a God-given responsibility to do what they can to prepare the Church for what may be ahead, even though it is a very unwelcome message? Our responsibility is to God, not to man.

Finally, pretribulationism is not essential to premillennialism. We would conclude by reinforcing the thesis for which we are pleading by quoting from several outstanding men of God. C. C. Ryrie, Professor of Theology at Dallas Theological Seminary: ". . . let it be said that one's attitude toward the tribulation or the rapture is not a decisive factor in premillennialism." "Premillennialism as a system is not dependent upon one's view of the rapture." "Premillennialism does not stand or fall on one's view of the tribulation. It is not the decisive issue."

Dr. Lewis Sperry Chafer: "Certain phases of prophecy find good men taking positions which are opposed the one to the other. The prophetic word has come plainly enough for all to agree on it, but just the same its meaning cannot always be ascertained to the satisfaction of all conservative minds. There is room for a difference of viewpoint on prophetic points where none exists in the realm of salvation truth, basic as that doctrine must be for all time."

President John Walvoord of Dallas Theological Seminary: "Before the first coming of the Lord, there was confusion even among the prophets concerning the distinction between the first and second comings (I Peter 1:10-11). At the present time, there is similar confusion between the translation of the church and the second coming to establish the millennial kingdom. An attitude of Christian tolerance is called for toward those who differ on this doctrine. But may we all 'love his appearing' " (II Tim. 4:8).

Dr. Charles E. Fuller said on the Old Fashioned Revival Hour, "A word of warning, sweetly given: do not make this difference a test of orthodoxy. Be tolerant in this matter. If a truly born again believer differs with you, don't withdraw your fellowship because of this difference on this matter; it is not a test of orthodoxy. Churches should not be divided over this point of doctrine. The test of orthodoxy, beloved — listen, and I will give my life for it — is based on the Virgin Birth, the Incarnation: God manifest in the flesh, the atoning sacrifice, the bodily resurrection of Christ from among the dead, His ascension, His intercession and His coming again. If a man bring any doctrine other than I have stated, receive him not into your home.

"It gives me grief to see the contention over some secondary — shall I put it — point of doctrine. Satan loves to divide and bring division in the body of believers. If you believe one point, or the second point, or the third point, of this pre-, mid- and posttribulation rapture, God bless you."

CONCLUSION

We have now concluded our study both of the Biblical teaching about the Blessed Hope and of the history of pretribulationism, and have come to the following conclusions. The idea of a pretribulation rapture was not seen in the Scriptures by the early church fathers. They were futurists and premillennialists but not pretribulationists. This of itself indicates that pretribulationism and premillennialism are not identical and that the Blessed Hope is not the hope of a rapture before the Tribulation. Pretribulationism was an unknown teaching until the rise of the Plymouth Brethren among whom the doctrine originated. From this source, it has come to America where, although warmly received by some, it has been rejected by other devout students of the Word, or has been at first accepted and later rejected by others. This very fact should suggest caution in making pretribulationism an essential element in prophetic interpretation.

The vocabulary of the Blessed Hope knows nothing of two aspects of Christ's coming, one secret and one glorious. On the contrary, the terminology points to a single indivisible return of Christ. Scripture says nothing about a secret coming of the Lord.

The Scriptures which predict the Great Tribulation, the Rapture and the Resurrection nowhere place the Rapture and the Resurrection of the saints at the beginning of the Tribulation. Nor does Scripture know anything of two phases of the first resurrection — that of the saints and that of the tribulation martyrs — separated by a seven-year period of tribulation. On the contrary, the one passage which is most specific as to chronology places the resurrection of both martyrs and saints after the Tribulation. Furthermore, the isolated verses which are

claimed for pretribulationism do not in fact assert a pretribulation rapture. This doctrine is nowhere affirmed
in the Word of God; it is an assumption in light of which
the Word is interpreted.

We have examined the arguments on which the assumption rests and have found that they do not require this
inference. Such terminology as that of Christ's coming
for and with His saints, the day of the Lord and the
day of Christ do not establish two events. Scripture says
nothing about a removal of the Holy Spirit. The Revelation says nothing about the Rapture and does not see a
raptured Church in heaven during the Tribulation. In
fact, the union of Christ with His bride does not take
place until His return after the Tribulation.

The Biblical teaching of watching is not the equivalent
of watching for an any-moment coming of Christ.

The Scriptures which promise deliverance from God's
wrath do not prove a pretribulation rapture, because God's
people who will find themselves on earth during the Tribulation will be divinely sheltered from the outpourings
of wrath. On the other hand, it would be a reversal of
God's providences in history if He were to remove the
Church from the last attack of human and satanic hostility even though it will be the worst history has known.

The concept that the Scriptures which refer to the Great
Tribulation have to do only with Israel and not with the
Church is an arbitrary method of interpreting the Word
which, if carried out consistently, would make havoc of
Biblical interpretation. We have found that dispensationalists themselves do not apply this method of "dividing the Word" in a consistent manner.

Finally, we concluded that the undue concern with the
question of pretribulationism tends to cause neglect of
more important and vital issues having to do with the
Blessed Hope; that it is not necessary for the preservation
of the purifying influence of the Blessed Hope; that it
tends to misunderstand the most fundamental element in

the purifying Hope; that it sacrifices one of the greatest incentives for world evangelization; that a Biblical attitude of expectancy is not identical with a belief in an any-moment coming of Christ; that it misrepresents the Blessed Hope by defining it in terms of escape from suffering rather than union with Christ and thus may be guilty of the positive danger of leaving the Church unprepared for tribulation when Antichrist appears; and that pretribulationism is not essential to a premillennial eschatology.

In short, pretribulationism is neither affirmed by the Word of God, nor is it an inference required by the Word, nor is it essential for the preservation of the highest spiritual values. It is, on the contrary, beset by certain grave dangers.

What is to be said of posttribulationism? Let it be here clearly affirmed that the author has no desire to be represented as a protagonist of posttribulationism, although this is probably inevitable. A Christian leader of national stature recently wrote, "One of these days you are going to be greatly surprised and you will be caught up to meet the Lord before the Tribulation breaks upon us. Don't you hope so?" To this question, we reply with an emphatic, Yes, we do. Let no one say that the author *wants* to see the Church suffer persecution or tribulation, or that he *desires* to find himself in the Great Tribulation. However, questions of theology are not decided by our desires or our dislikes; they are decided by appeal to the Word of God. And since we do not find pretribulationism taught in the Word of God, we must insist that this position should not claim that it is synonymous with the Blessed Hope. The author has frequently heard the reaction expressed both by laymen and pastors that they believe in a pretribulation rapture because they do not want to suffer the Great Tribulation. Who does desire it? However, the question is, What saith the Word? And unless the Word is clear on such an important point, can we run the risk of promising God's people what may be a false security of deliverance from trouble when what they need is warning and preparation to endure trouble?

The question will be asked, Does the Word assert that the Church *will* go through the Tribulation? Is not post-tribulationism equally an inference? Is the student of the Word to throw up his hands and make an arbitrary choice between two inferences, selecting the one he prefers?

With the exception of one passage, the author will grant that the Scripture nowhere explicitly states that the Church will go through the Great Tribulation. God's people are seen in the Tribulation, but they are not called the Church but the elect or the saints. Nor does the Word explicitly place the Rapture at the end of the Tribulation. Most of the references to these final events lack chronological indications. Perhaps God wishes us to be certain about the great verities of Christ's return, the Rapture and the Resurrection, but has deliberately refrained from answering all of our questions as to the order of events. However, in one passage, Revelation 20, the Resurrection is placed at the return of Christ in glory. This is more than an inference. Furthermore, even apart from the clear teaching of Revelation, if we were left only to inference, our study has suggested that a single indivisible return of Christ, which requires a posttribulation view, is the inference which is more naturally suggested than that of two comings of Christ with a pretribulation rapture.

The author takes it as a basic hermeneutical principle that in disputed questions of interpretation, the simpler view is to be preferred; *the burden of proof rests upon the more elaborate explanation.* We know that Christ is coming back in power and great glory. We know that every eye shall see Him for He shall come as lightning blazes from one end of heaven to the other. We know that when He comes, the dead in Christ will be raised, the living saints will be raptured, Antichrist will be judged, and the millennial kingdom inaugurated. If the Coming of

Christ, the Resurrection and the Rapture are not a single indivisible event followed immediately thereafter by the punishment of Antichrist and the inauguration of the kingdom, the burden of proof rests on those who would elaborate this basic outline by dividing the coming of Christ into two aspects and the first resurrection into two parts. Unless such a proof is forthcoming, the necessary inference is that this division of the coming of Christ and the resurrection into two parts is invalid, and one is not required to accept it as the teaching of the Word of God. Students and teachers of the Word may hold this position if they feel it helps them to understand the Scriptures, but they ought not insist that this doctrine is essential to sound doctrine and an indispensable element in premillennial eschatology. It should be held as a teaching about which there may be legitimate differences of opinion within the area of prophetic interpretation.

The analogy has been drawn between the prophetic expectation of the first coming of Christ and our expectation of His second coming. We have quoted Dr. Walvoord to the effect that "before the first coming of the Lord, there was confusion even among the prophets concerning the distinction between the first and second comings (I Peter 1:10-11)." The prophets were not given sufficient light to make an accurate detailed chart of prophetic events. The distinction between the two advents of Christ could not be appreciated until He came the first time. If the analogy holds, God has not even now given us enough light to make an accurate, detailed chart of all the events which will attend the second advent. Jesus did not criticize the disciples for failing to have a correct interpretation of the Old Testament prophecies *before the event* but only for failure to recognize the fulfillment when it actually occurred.

Following this analogy, we must conclude that there could be distinctions involved in events attending Christ's return, but *these distinctions will not become really clear until the events themselves actually take place*. Meanwhile, we must insist that the contemporary inference of two aspects in the second coming does not have the explicit confirmation of Scripture. The natural interpretation of the return of Christ is that of a single glorious event at the very end; and this was always the expectation of the futurist views of the Church until the creation of the dispensational distinctions. The burden of proof rests upon those who insist that the natural and simplest explanation is not the Biblical teaching. Pretribulationism is not asserted in the Scripture; it is not proven. It is an assumption in light of which Scriptures are interpreted. The strong balance of probability rests with the simpler view, especially since this view is not burdened by contradictions.

Having said this, we would revert to our original thesis, only to broaden it: neither pretribulationism nor posttribulationism should be made a ground of fellowship, a test of orthodoxy, or a necessary element in Christian doctrine. There should be liberty and charity toward both views. That which is essential is the expectation of "the blessed hope and appearing of the glory of our great God and Saviour Jesus Christ."